When you read the words and teachings within, you are reading the words of the Masters in the World of Spirit, or Heaven as we know it. The teachings, like the words of the great Prophets of the past, have been sent to the Earth plane now, so that mankind can assist in changing the World into the place that it was always meant to be.

Maitreya, the Ascended Masters and God, The Creator, have sent these messages for every single person on the Earth plane irrespective of race, colour, gender and rank, religious or political persuasion. They are for all mankind equally.

The messages of the past are in the past. These are the messages for the Now.

Previously published by:
SPIRITUAL PHILOSOPHY PUBLISHING LIMITED

SOME SILENT HERO

Coming Soon

THE CHIEF'S FORGOTTEN LAND
STEPPING STONES
MAITREYA VOLUME TWO

Maitreya

Teachings from Heaven

–Volume One–

Channelled by

Margaret Birkin

SPIRITUAL PHILOSOPHY PUBLISHING LIMITED

ℳaitreya

Published by:
Spiritual Philosophy Publishing Limited
PO Box 79
Midhurst
West Sussex
GU29 9WW

Spiritual Philosophy Publishing website:
www.spiritualphilosophy.co.uk

British Library Cataloguing in Publication Data.
A catalogue record for this book is available from the
British Library.

ISBN 0-9548959-1-6

Printed and bound by Cambridge University Press.
Typesetting by Cecil Smith.
Cover design by Ian Tyrrell of RPM, Chichester.

The publisher wishes to thank every individual and
company that has helped put this book into print.

Contents

Acknowledgements 1
PREFACE
What is Channelling? 3
USING THIS BOOK 5
MAITREYA'S
TEACHINGS A-Z 7
ABUNDANCE 7
A MESSAGE TO ALL
THOSE WHO BELONG
TO RELIGIOUS GROUPS 9
ANGER 10
ANIMALS AND PLANTS
AND KARMA 13
ASCENSION 14
ASTROLOGY 17
AVOIDING DARKNESS 18
AWARENESS 20
BEAUTY 20
CHILDREN 22
CHOICE 23
CHOICE (II) 25
CHOICES 27
COLOUR 28
COLOUR (II) 29
COMPLEMENTARY
MEDICINE 30
CONDITIONING 31
CONFLICT 33
CONSIDERATION
FOR OTHERS 34
CONTROL 36
CRITICISM 37
DEPRESSION 38
DIFFERENCES 39
DIFFERENCES (II) 41
DISCERNMENT
AND THE TRUTH 42
DISCIPLINE & SPIRITUAL
DEVELOPMENT 43
EMOTIONS 45
ENEMIES 45
ENERGY 46
EUTHANASIA 48
EVERYONE HAS A HEART 50
EXCESS BAGGAGE 51

FAMILY 51
FEAR 55
FREEING THE SOUL
FROM FEAR 56
GOD DOES NOT WANT
US TO SUFFER 57
HAPPINESS 58
HEAVEN on EARTH 60
HOW CAN I SERVE
HUMANITY? 61
HOW TO BE
TRULY SPIRITUAL 63
HOW WE COMMUNICATE
WITH YOU 64
INDEPENDENCE 67
INTUITION 69
JUDGEMENT 70
KARMA 71
KILLING 75
LESSONS 76
LOVE 77
MARRIAGE 79
MILLENNIUM CHANGES 80
MIRRORS 81
MONEY 83
MY ARRIVAL 85
MY ARRIVAL IN
CONNECTION WITH
THE RAPTURE 86
NATURE 88
NOW 89
OPINIONS 91
PAIN 92
PAST 94
PAST LIFE
INCARNATIONS 95
PAST LIVES 97
PATIENCE 98
PEACE 99
PEACE (II) 102
POSSESSIONS 103
PROPHETS 105
PUT GOD FIRST 109
QUESTIONING 109
RELIGION 110

RESPECT	111	VIRUSES	171
SEXUALITY	112	WAR	172
SILENCE		WEIGHT LOSS	173
(Listen to your Soul)	114	WHAT ARE ANIMALS?	176
SO YOU PROFESS TO		WHAT DO I THINK OF	
BE SPIRITUAL	116	RELIGION?	178
SOUL GROWTH	117	WHAT DO WE DO?	179
SPIRITUAL LAW	118	WHAT HAPPENS	
SPIRITUAL WRITINGS	120	WHEN YOU PRAY? (1)	180
SPIRITUALITY	121	WHAT HAPPENS	
SPIRITUALITY AND		WHEN YOU PRAY? (11)	182
SEXUAL ENERGY	122	WHAT HAPPENS	
SUFFERING	124	WHEN YOU PRAY? (111)	183
SURROGACY	127	WHAT IS LOVE?	184
TALK	128	WHO is GOD?	185
THE ANTI-CHRIST	130	WHY DO I ONLY	
THE CHRIST SOUL	131	SPEAK ENGLISH?	186
THE EMOTIONAL BODY		WHY DO YOU	
(ASTRAL BODY)	133	HAVE FEAR?	187
THE GRINDSTONE	134	WHY DO YOU LIE	
THE MAIN LIFE LESSON	135	TO YOURSELF?	189
THE MASTERS	137	WHY I AM CALLED	
THE NEW MILLENNIUM	140	'LORD MAITREYA'	190
THE NEW		WHY ME?	191
MILLENNIUM 2000	142	WHY NATURAL	
THE PAST	144	DISASTERS?	193
THE PHYSICAL BODY	145	WHY NEW ZEALAND?	194
The Problem of		WORKING WITH	
Becoming Spiritual		THE MASTERS	195
Using Your Brain	147	WORRY	197
THE PURPOSE OF LIFE	149	YOU ARE ON A JOURNEY	198
THE PURPOSE		YOU CANNOT TAKE	
OF THE SOUL	150	ANYTHING WITH YOU	199
THE SELF (Ego) and		YOUR FEAR!	200
the HIGHER SELF		YOUR LIFE JOURNEY!	201
(Spiritual)	151		
THE SOUL	156	APPENDICES	203
THEOSOPHY	157	APPENDIX 1	
THOUGHT ENERGY	158	Transcript of the	
TIME	160	United Nations SEAT	
TIME FOR CHANGE	161	Speech by Maitreya	205
TITHING	162	APPENDIX 2	
TOUCHING AND		DISASTER IN THE USA	
PERSONAL CONTACT	164	and THE HALL OF	
TRANSPLANTED		MIRRORS – Re: 9/11	215
BODY ORGANS	165	GLOSSARY	217
TRUST	167	SPIRITUAL PHILOSOPHY	
TRUTH	168	PUBLISHING	219
UPDATE ON THE		MAITREYA WEBSITE	221
PHOTON BELT	170	UPCOMING TITLES	224

Acknowledgements

I would like to acknowledge the following people who have helped me on my spiritual path:

Peter Luke for all his assistance in creating the website and helping me through many difficult years of spiritual development. My family for their love and support of a mother who is different to most mothers!

My partner Alan McElroy for his support and love and to my spiritual Master, Maitreya, for helping me climb the stairs! (This is something the Master knows about)

Ratna Collaru and Mark King for their continuous work on the website in posting channelling and their support of the Master's work.

PREFACE

What is Channelling?
…Spirit took over the writing from here

"Since the earliest records of Prophets, Sages and the great wisdoms of Abraham, people through the ages have channelled the messages given to them by Spirit.

But who is Spirit?

It may seem odd, but it is truth that Spirit has guided, moulded and shaped every step of the human path and the human condition. We in Spirit want to teach our Earth bound friends about the wisdoms of a higher calling, the messages from God. It is He/She that sends this message to you today.

Look at your life, just yours, no one else's and think, 'How can I make this better?' The answer is to get in touch with the spiritual person that you are. You are an incredible being, full of life and pain and resource; yet the one thing, let's call it a quality, that separates you from everything around you is the individuality of your spirit. There is no one else on this earth like you. You are at one with God, your father. Choose to be the person, the wonderful creation that you are.

Connect with Spirit, quieten, listen and eventually when

you are ready, Spirit will talk with you, guide you, love you and that is channelling: your own connection with God, the life force of the Universe. God bless you, everyone."

Inspirational Writing

"Inspirational writing is a gift. It is heaven sent. It is available to anyone bold enough to open their hearts and minds so that Spirit can connect with your Higher Self; your Soul. Generations of enlightened people have sought the words of God and the Higher Realms. It is through us that man connects with Heaven. Let us help you on your journey. When you eventually connect in this way, all things on Earth are possible to every person that wants to talk to us. Enjoy every moment of every day; this is your chance to have a chat."

Learning to channel

"Everyone can channel, from children to old age. Channelling is a matter of opening up your telephone lines so that we can talk to you. It occurs at a higher vibrational frequency that normal thought, so by tuning into our frequency you can talk to us and reveal your innermost thoughts on any subject in the world. We are ready and waiting for your call."

This Preface was channelled by the Publisher.

USING THIS BOOK

T he hardest part of being a human being is making sense of the world around us. What would God say about fear, depression, wars, marriage, euthanasia, women, surrogacy, homosexuality, religion and our purpose for being here on the Earth? If only we could talk to God, world poverty would cease to exist, or would it?

All things can change if there is a will. We all have choice in our lives. We can be a robber, a thief, a nurse or a doctor, a street cleaner or the Pope. All these things are down to us as individuals; we have a choice. We can be whatever we want to be and we can do whatever we want to do. We have that choice.

Most of us want something better in life. Our Government cannot do it for us, only we can achieve our life ambitions.

In this book you will read the words of Maitreya.

- Maitreya is an Ascended Master and one step below God. Many people call him the World Teacher, but these are labels given by man. He is a messenger. The messages within this book are given with love to help mankind onto the next stages of human development and evolution.

Each Teaching, each beautiful philosophy is divine in its simplicity. Each lesson can be learnt by everyone from beggarman to world leader. Philosophy from spirit knows

5

nothing of rank or wealth, or position. These philosophies are given to everyone, irrespective of race, religion, colour, age or sex.

When you apply these wisdoms to yourself, your life *will* change, and for the betterment of all mankind.

Maitreya's Teachings A–Z
ABUNDANCE

" ou were all meant to have abundance in your life. *Yes, every one of you!*

Yet, you do not know of this and many of you stop the flow to that abundance by your thinking. There is a common conception that some people are born to abundance and others have to suffer. This is not true. The Creator made you all the same. *All of you* can have abundance in your life; you just need to create it. Yes, some of you have lessons to learn about this subject and may find it harder than others to create this, but it should not be a problem and you will find that abundance.

You waste so much Earth time by living in the past, not believing in yourself, having doubts about your abilities, etc. You *cannot* change what has been, why concern yourself with it? When you let go of the past, you can create the future in a far better way. The energy is there to assist you because it is not being wasted on the past. The abundance that is yours by right can start to enter your life in whatever way you have manifested it.

There are those who think that abundance is wrong; that one should not have abundance. How can one attain the things one wants if one does not have abundance? Think of what one can do if one has the means; it makes for a lovely life.

There is nothing wrong with abundance, it is what you do

7

with it that counts. Think about where in your life you would like abundance and then let go of all negative thinking concerning that area. Then watch as your life changes. It really is very simple."

A MESSAGE TO ALL THOSE WHO BELONG TO RELIGIOUS GROUPS

"I have been aware of the negative emails that my channel has been receiving since she started, at my request, this website. Some of those souls who have written profess to be Christians and other religious groups.

The purpose of all religions is to bring the word *Love* into the world.

Since the beginning of time, there have been many messengers of God. Each one of them has interpreted the word of God in their own way.

My question to you is, 'Why are you so angry? Why do you hate so?'

If you belong to Christian, Jew, Moslem, or any other religious group, why do you persecute one who comes with the message of *Love* for *this* age?

There is nothing in my writings which speak of the negative. The writings are created to uplift humanity; to help those souls who are searching for the spiritual, but who do not wish to belong to a group. How can this be wrong? If you are spiritual, really truly spiritual, you will have only *Love* in your heart, and all hatred, anger and fear will no longer be there."

9

ANGER

by Dwjhal Kuhl – The Tibetan Master

Guest of the Master Maitreya

" *I* wish to write on the subject of anger and what it is doing to humanity in general. As you can see, it is becoming very destructive in its expression. Why is this happening and what can we do lessen it, or reduce it?

The night after the High School shooting (in Littleton, Denver, Colorado, USA, April 1999), where a number of young people died and passed away from the Earth Plane, I took my disciple* and blended his consciousness with the main person responsible for what happened. I might say he found the experience very unpleasant indeed. He felt and thought what the young men were feeling and thinking at the time of the killings.

After coming back from the Astral Plane into his physical body and waking up, he felt very sick. It took him some time to come to grips with what he experienced while out of the body. As his teacher, I asked him what his thoughts were now that he knew what went on in the mind of the killers. He had just one answer, '*Anger!*' anger to an almost unbelievable level.

10

* *Dwjhal Kuhl is channelled by Peter Luke who is the Webmaster for the Maitreya Education Trust website.*

Where does this anger come from, that such a lot of people around the world are experiencing? And why is it being so destructive?

For a start, a lot of anger that people feel does not come from this incarnation at all. It comes from many past lives. Past lives where things have gone wrong and anger is felt and not dealt with. After all, anger is a negative energy and energy cannot be destroyed, it can only be transmuted. The best of all being into love.

There are millions of people living on the Earth Plane at this time that have vast amounts of anger from past lives that has not been dealt with and transmuted. It only takes something small to trigger this past life negativity off, and rage is the result.

For instance, someone may be driving along the road quite happily, feeling not too bad, except perhaps a little stressed out. Another driver, who is having a rather difficult day, cuts in front of our driver causing him to brake hard, or maybe even clipping his car. This minor happening could easily cause what you call 'road rage' in a driver who hadn't dealt with his anger in past lives.

The road rage that a driver displays is only stored up negative energy that has suddenly found an outlet. Road rage and other negative outbursts or temper, will continue to be displayed in a person, until he has dealt with all negative energy. Whether it is from past incarnations, the present life or both.

Most people have no idea that this time bomb of anger is just sitting below the surface waiting to go off. When it does explode, disaster is the result. There has been no education in this area at all, either by the church or social services of most countries. Hence, there are more time bombs than you can ever imagine.

Unfortunately, negativity and anger has been increased many fold by other factors. Factors such as violent films (movies), violent contact and blood sports, all add to the anger in an individual. All these forces become cumulative until the person can no longer contain them, then the bomb goes off. The High School shooting was the effect of such a person not being able to handle the negativity before anyone could recognize the danger signals.

When you have a big group of people who have anger, then a collective unconsciousness forms where wars can start and killing on a large scale can happen. Kosovo is an example of this unconsciousness working.

What can be done about this anger to defuse it?

Counselling with a past life therapist and one who is versed in the matters of spiritual realms can go a long way to helping an individual gain balance and poise once more. It is not an easy road to take, but it must be taken if the person is to get better without creating much negative karma. Once counselling and past life therapy is started, other avenues will open up for further help.

I leave these thoughts with you."

Dwjhal Kuhl

ANIMALS AND PLANTS
AND KARMA

"I am often asked, 'Master, do animals have souls and do they incur karma?' This is indeed so. Every living thing has a soul, from the tree in the park to the dog in the kennel. Of course, their souls are not as advanced as those of humans, but nevertheless, they have a soul. For each action, there is a reaction. With the tree, there can be little karma for a tree is immobile and cannot move. The patterns of its cycles, through the years, usually stay stable. However, it lives and breathes, moving and growing each year. A tree dies many times in one human lifetime. It dies in winter, shedding its leaves and in spring it is revived, growing new shoots, perhaps growing fruit or flower. Then again dying, and again being re-born. Year in, year out, this cycle continues. This is so with all the plant kingdom. They do not die, they just move on again, sometimes improving themselves, sometimes not. For this species there is little or no karma, just a cycle of life.

For the animals too, there is a cycle of life. However, their cycle is not so long as the tree, plant or flower. They incarnate just as humans do. They have souls just as humans do. Animals have a survival instinct just as humans do. Just as in the human kingdom there is reaction to every action, so there is too with animals. It may surprise many souls to know that certain animals incarnate to be companions to certain souls. They come for that specific purpose. What is given out must come back; it is the law of the Universe.

13

Animals do incur karma. For instance, my channel has a

cat, a very beautiful Persian breed that she saved from the sleep needle at the local animal shelter. This animal came to be a companion to them. In one house they lived in, this cat had a habit of visiting the neighbour (where they too had a cat) and raiding the other cat's food bowl. When they moved to another home, *he* became the cat whose food bowl was raided. A local cat decided to visit the house and steal *his* food, just as he had done in the previous home. As you give out, so you get back! Reaction against action.

This cycle of karmic energy will not be ended until both cats realize the energy they are putting into the action. It may not end until they both evolve into the human kingdom, for that is where animals move on to. How many times have you said to yourself, 'that dog is human' on seeing an animal so intelligent it defies belief. That animal will probably evolve in its next incarnation to a human. These souls evolve as very basic humans, but nevertheless, their souls take on human form and then start the climb onward to more and more intelligence, understanding and spirituality. Animals create karma just as humans do. There is no difference."

ASCENSION

"For many years, many people on the Earth plane have talked about ascension. Many have said that space beings will come to the Earth plane and take the good souls away. Others have predicted that only certain church groups will ascend when the Christ Soul returns. The real truth is that all mankind can ascend. However, many souls will *not*, because they will *not* raise their vibration.

The Photon Belt energy, the Christ Spirit, is aiding to raise the vibration of those on this planet. Many souls will not be able to handle the higher energy unless they have cleared away their blockages and dealt with controlling the physical, emotional, mental and spiritual bodies. Millions of souls on this Earth plane have been trapped, returning incarnation after incarnation, unable to leave this vibration because of their lack of knowledge about the chakras and their purpose. They lack the knowledge of past life memory and keep themselves in darkness, only achieving nirvana or peace between life times. They have to return over and over trying to clear away the dross of incarnation after incarnation.

The Christ Soul came through Jesus 2000 years ago. He was a medium and healer. He transfigured, just as many mediums do today, and brought with him the Photon Belt energy then. Today it is being done again to help humankind raise their vibration. Sadly, the words of the teacher Jesus have been changed beyond their original meaning. Many other prophets have also spoken and brought new energy and messages from the Masters to aid mankind, but all of them have been interpreted wrongly.

The message is being given again
in the hope that humankind will listen.

For those who have sought spiritual help, who are without negative conditioning and thought; for those that have love for their fellow human, despite their failings, and for those who follow the light and have no judgment of another, they will finally leave this Earth plane never to

15

return. They will move to a higher vibration away from the negativity, and they will be at one with the Supreme Being or God. This will happen for all souls who are in this present incarnation and who have raised their vibration. Those who do not raise their vibration and who do not heed the message of the Masters, *they* will stay Earth-bound once again, to incarnate over and over for another one thousand years of Earth time, until another energy comes to transform and aid those who want to leave.

Many of those leaving the Earth plane this time are attached to the Space Brotherhood of many incarnations past. They came to seed and to teach. But once they blended their energy with that of humankind on Earth their Higher Self, that was of the purest and highest, merged with the Self of the primitive man. The animal part of humankind and subsequent offspring, was tied to the Earth plane; incarnating life after life, trying to free itself from the Self; trying desperately to merge with the Higher Self, but unable to do so because the vibration of the planet was not high enough.

That is now changing and humankind has the opportunity to change. The dark forces are gathering also, waiting to pounce on those who want to change. Many will succumb to temptation and go backwards, but many will move forward onto Ascension, and the merging with God of the Divine Soul, to leave the Earth plane forever.

There is so little time, and many souls to contact. Many words have already been spoken and written but still, humankind bury their heads in the sand. Many channels have been sent and remain unheard because humankind has come to love the darkness and has forgotten what the light is like. It is not the singing of hymns and the chanting of prayers. Nor is it the insistence on following one particular sect or cult or doing things a particular way. It is in being honest with oneself, facing one's negative or dark side, seeing good in every soul, never judging another. It is a peace that passes all understanding.

Let yourself be led to the Light, let the Light shine through, and the reward will be that peace. Let yourself be led away from the Earth plane to Ascension; to a higher vibration and to a union that is beyond anything you have ever known. It can start now. You can experience that peace. You just have to turn to the Light, be free of all criticism, judgment of another, free of the emotional body, understand the spiritual laws and abide by them. Love your fellow man with all your heart, and be willing to grow spiritually. The opening of this door is not easy.

We have sent many teachers to help you; they are everywhere. And, if you ask, you will be led to them. It means facing your Self, and letting it go. Then will you make ascension to the higher vibration."

ASTROLOGY

"Often you say to yourself, 'How can I find what my life lessons are? How can I attain the ladder to a higher vibration?' This is very easy if you have the keys to the correct knowledge, because it is all connected to spiritual astrology. Only when you can learn of your life path through astrology, can you start to work to attain higher levels of awareness.

In your natal chart are all the answers to your very being;

17

to your life lessons and to those lessons you have brought back with you to learn again. You cannot move forward spiritually until you become aware of this. You can become a great healer or psychic with all the knowledge that you learn, however, if you are not aware of your life lessons, you cannot move to a higher vibration.

Astrology to some has been so complicated that they have shied away from it. But with the advent of computers in the world today, it is becoming easy to produce information based on the natal chart; the life plan, as we call it, *you chose* to bring with you. Once you understand the knowledge of astrology, then you have the keys to raising your vibration. Every soul has a life plan. Some astrologers do not deal with spiritual astrology, so, often valuable information is omitted when you are given a chart.

What have you chosen to learn in this incarnation? Find your life lessons and you will find your answers. It is as simple as that."

AVOIDING DARKNESS

" hat is darkness? Many souls are afraid of, 'the dark side.' Who are the dark side and what do they do? The dark side is your *Self*. It is your own fear and insecurity. There is no devil, nor is there a dark side, these come from within yourself. If you have fear, then you will draw that which you fear into your aura. It will come in the form of many things. It can be manifested on its own, through your close associates and family, but it will manifest if you fear it.

Other people's fears can become your own. Certain souls who are destined to become healers can, from an early childhood age, absorb the negativity of others, especially family. This can, in turn, manifest in the person at any time in their life.

If you give others no power, they have no power over you. If a person makes you feel fearful, look into the past, either this life or others, for this is where the fear comes from. If other people around you are negative, then work constantly to uplift their spirits. It is surprising, that if you are positive and they are negative, their negativity will either be swayed by you being so positive, or they will not be able to bear it and will move away.

Humanity has a habit of getting involved in the affairs of others. You interfere so many times when you should not. By doing this, you do not realize that the one you are helping is not helping themselves and so, in effect, you stop that soul from growing. It is possible for *your* actions in helping, to bring the soul back for another round of incarnation! Each soul has their own script which was created before they were born, and like the actors on a stage, they are acting out their script. Everyone around them is their supporting cast, who are helping the person to live that script.

Nothing is real, all is illusion, but until you can raise your vibration away from the Earth plane and move into detachments, you will never see this. You are the creator of your own reality. You can choose the light or the dark, the positive or the negative. You choose. Which one do you want?"

AWARENESS

"I have been asked many times, 'Master what can I do to become more spiritual?' and I say to the soul, 'be aware.'

Be aware of what you are saying to others, and of how you say it. Be aware of the words coming out of your mouth. Be aware of how your *Self* manipulates you, *not to do* the very thing you know will raise your vibration. It is not easy being on the spiritual path, for as you move forwards in energy, the Earth plane energy will try to draw you back into the fold that you have just left. Nobody is perfect, and moving up in vibration is not an easy task. It can be made easier though, with *you* becoming aware of everything you do, and of *how* you try and sabotage yourself as you grow. It can often be a case of two steps forward, one step back. As you move though, and keep on moving, you can gradually move away from the Earth plane, and find a peace that many have never experienced. It is worth striving for."

BEAUTY

"I have mentioned, in many communications, about humankind each having a different vibration. I write to you now about the subject of beauty and of it being *within* and not *without*.

Many souls on the Earth plane are concerned about their beauty. Whether they have the right body, a beautiful figure, too many facial lines etc, and this applies to men as well as women. They cannot often see the beauty that is within. The beauty of the soul.

When you are at peace, and happy with yourself, then one does not concern oneself with mundane thinking. The body that you have is only on loan for this lifetime and it is one you have chosen. The shape of your body, face and appearance, is all due to genetic programming from many members of your families.

Your soul however is not genetic, but is your own, created from your own lessons, experiences and growth in the spiritual realms. When your soul is at peace, *you* are at peace. This manifests as a beautiful glow around the body; your energy is golden. It does not matter what you 'look like' as those who look at you see the face of God.

My channel Margaret often despaired because she carried extra weight. She was once very thin, but as she matured she gained weight. I have informed her that she could not take the energy of the spiritual world if she did not have some measure of protection. Thankfully, since raising her vibration, she has let go of the need to be 'beautiful' externally, and has become 'beautiful' internally.

The more you open to love and the divine energy, and deal with your blocks and fears, the more you can become a beautiful channel for the divine light; that golden, beautiful light of God or the Divine Soul. Beauty then shines from within. The external part of you is not seen because of the beautiful vision from within. All those who come into your energy see that beauty and cease to look at the external.

They do not see your crooked nose, your body with extra weight, your blemishes and what you consider to be flaws. All they see is the beauty of the Divine Soul or God. The desire for beauty is the desire of the Self. Once you

21

surpass that desire, once the Higher Self is attained through dealing with your own limitations, blocks, fears, desires, doubts and insecurities, then you can shine from within and all that shines is beauty, a golden light which then becomes radiant.

Beauty is not *without*; only the Self sees that and complains. Beauty is *within*, and when it is allowed to shine and come forth, then it can become a beautiful energy to see and to mirror for everyone else."

CHILDREN

"*Y*our children are only in your care. *They* choose *you* as their parent, for the lessons you will help them to learn. You are often the catalyst for their experiences. Many children are young adults; even while still very young, people comment on them as, 'old souls' or of, 'being here before.'

At an early age, depending on the child, the child should be encouraged to do everything for themselves. *So many parents* try to do it for the child perhaps, because of their own childhood being so hard; they want to help their own child avoid the life they had. However, when one helps a child to do something they can do for themselves, one stops that child's growth. Each soul comes into an incarnation with the skills to learn all they need for their growth. Often, the parents think because they are children they need parental guidance, and yes, they do. But children need to learn from their *own* experiences, *not* from those of the parents. Children are far more resilient than adults. They can cope with the most difficult of circumstances because they have nothing else to judge it upon. To them, difficult circumstances are normal. Only adults say, 'you can't do that,' and by saying that, they stop the child from learning the lesson of the action.

I was once asked when a child should start to make their own decisions and I told this soul, five years of age is when a child should start making their own decisions. By doing this, they can select their own life, *not that* which their parents chose. So many children are pushed into doing things they do not want to do because, 'Mother (or father) wanted me to do that.'

Each child is programmed astrologically to find their own lessons and to fulfil their destiny. Adults stop that from happening. If a child is allowed to go with the flow, they will be led and guided to where they have to go. The right circumstances will come to them to enable them to fulfil their destiny. If you, as an adult, stop that from happening, you will stop the growth of your child. Let your child go and see the evolvement of that soul. This *does not* mean that there should not be discipline or rules in the home, these are very important, but each child should be allowed to choose their own destiny and how they fulfil it."

CHOICE

" hy do you have choice? You have choice so that you can choose for yourself which direction you will take with your life. *You* are responsible for your own life. *Nobody else* has your life plan; has chosen your life lessons or the opportunities and possibilities which lie in front of you. *You alone* make the choice.

There are many instances on the Earth plane where choice has created war, pain, hurt and even killing. For instance, when a woman finds herself with child and makes the choice not to keep it but to have the pregnancy terminated, it is *her* choice! Nobody has the right to judge her except the energy of the God force.

She may have chosen this experience to learn lessons from. She may have to go through the experience to help the soul who was coming in. Some souls are not even born; they just have to touch the Earth plane to finish their karma on it. Some women choose to be the vehicles for these souls, to enable them to return and enable this to happen.

When is a baby, a baby? It is a baby from the moment of quickening. That is when the soul enters the body. It is then that the soul is permanently attached. Until that moment in the fourth month of pregnancy, it is just an egg waiting for a soul. Even after that time a woman can lose a child, but it is by choice again, or, the fact that the soul entering decides not to continue.

This is just one example of choice. There are many examples. Each of you has the choice to create your life the way you want it. You are the sculptor, choice is your chisel."

CHOICE (II)

"You ou were created so that you may have choice. Each one of you can take many paths. You are born with a plan, a map you could perhaps say. That map/plan is your astrology chart. That plan can take you into many routes or directions. *You* make the choice.

Only when you become enlightened and choose to fulfil your spiritual destiny, do things change. When you are on the path of normal life, without spiritual development, your choices do not cause too much harm to yourself, although they are important. However, when you choose to fulfil your spiritual destiny then we, in Spirit, come in to help you.

The choices you make become more important. It is usually at this Earth time when souls choose not to go forward. Spiritual development is one of the hardest things to do. Each soul chooses how they will learn *their* lessons. Some choose to suffer humiliation, some to lose those close to them. Others choose that life will become difficult for them. *Each soul* makes their own choices. We just bring the souls into your life to help you learn. Often this is connected to karma. They (the souls) are programmed to do exactly what is needed for you to learn.

For instance, my channel had to learn lessons of ego. Her friend, who was also intuitive, told her that she would go to America to 'read' famous people and film stars. This was bait to her ego to get her to go, because in past incarnations she had only been interested in fame and fortune. This was designed to test her, to see if she would take the bait again. She took the bait!

25

Things were designed in America to see if she would take the same path. Doors closed on her and her ego was shredded to pieces. She was tempted by those with money and position, but in this incarnation they could not touch her and she did not take the old path. She passed her test. When she had done this, then we gave her the keys to her future; the key to work with us. Had she been tempted and gone with these offers, she would have still made good, but would not have been connected to us, the Masters. She made the choice. It was then, after this experience, and *only* then, that we gave instructions for this website.

Those who are your enemies on this Earth plane are often your best friend in other dimensions. They come to the Earth plane to help you to grow. Your choices decide your future. Each one of you will be tested to see your worthiness to work with us. This *has* to be done. *You* make the choice before you are born. The more emotional energy you give to situations, the more you stop your spiritual growth. It is often difficult to make the right choice, because the Self says one thing and the Higher Self another. Yet, when one lets go and separates from the situation, then the way is shown and which choice to make. Often this means letting go of people you love, the things you own, yet the more you let go, the more you grow.

Yes it is painful, but remember, the illusion is that these people are real; these situations also, but they are not. They are only created for you to learn. Your husband/ wife/partner now, will not be your husband in the world of Spirit, he/she will just be another soul. In another incarnation that person could be your son/father/friend.

When you raise your vibration you see beyond the illusion, you see life as it really is, an illusion.

The choices *you* make decide whether you grow in Spirit or not."

CHOICES

"ou think that life is pre-destined, and to a degree it is. But, it is also open to choice, not only your choice, but that of others too.

Life is filled with opportunities and possibilities, each one of them reliant on the actions of another. If everyone followed their plan, if everyone co-ordinated with every-one else, the world would be a better place.

But humanity chose to have choice, and because of this, a couple *may be destined* to be together, but one of the partners makes a choice, because of the *Self* or other reasons, *not* to stay. Something may be meant to happen, but someone's choice will stop it from happening. You may personally make a choice *not* to follow a certain path.

Nothing is pre-destined; it is all up to choice. The choices you make fashion your reality for tomorrow. There are never any mistakes either; everything is perfect in the Universe. It is just humanity that cannot see that perfection.

The next time you make a choice about something, ask yourself what will it do to the plans of another? What influence will it have on the future? By doing this you will come to understand choice and be more selective in your choosing.

27

You make the choices, not we. We are just here to guide you, teach you and help you as you make the pilgrim's progress through the lessons of your life."

COLOUR

"You do not realize how important colour is in your life. If only you did, you would wear the most wonderfully coloured clothes.

Each colour has a vibration and responds to the eyes of the one who looks at it. Did you also know that even the blind can be influenced by colour? Yes, this is so. For they *feel* the colour. They may not see it, but that does not mean they cannot *feel* it! All colour has a vibration, this is the reason the blind can *feel* the colour.

The colour red can bring in energy; it can also bring anger to the surface. The colour yellow can bring the most depressed person out of their depression enough to make them want to talk. It is the most wonderful colour for this. The colours that you wear and that you choose are a barometer to your soul. For those who wear black, it is not a morbid colour, it is neutral, but when worn with another colour such as blue, green, or turquoise, can become a wonderful healing colour for those who wear it and those who see it. The colour black enhances the other colours and makes it more profound, more striking.

Go into your heart and ask yourself, 'What colour would I really like to wear?' And no matter what that colour, wear it. If you do, you will be soothing your soul, and healing your mind, body and soul. Your soul knows what colour it needs, you just have to listen."

COLOUR (II)

"You do not realize *how* important colour is to your life. How, just having your own personal colour around you can not only lift your soul, but help you grow spiritually as well.

How do you know what your personal colour is? Some souls have only one particular colour, others have more than one. It is not uncommon for a soul to have three or four personal colours. Your personal colour is the one which you feel most comfortable with.

Many souls just tend to purchase clothes in their favourite colour, yet, surrounding yourself with the energy of your colour can also help you in an incredible way. The rays of your colour are designed to lift your spirits, aid you in your development and revitalize you. Having them around you can do so much to help you on your spiritual journey. Put the colours you like all around you and you will notice a change in your life. You will become more aware.

Light energy can penetrate these colours and just as they do with the flowers and trees in nature, they can also do the same with you. There are many ways to use colour around you; experiment, allow the colour to speak to you and tell you where it wants to be. Spend more time with colour and you will feel a difference. It can be healing, uplifting and intuitive."

COMPLEMENTARY MEDICINE

"If one is happy and content in one's life and at total peace with oneself, then there should be no illness. Illness comes from being at *dis-ease* with oneself.

Much has been written about complementary medicine and how it should be used. Many souls believe that this kind of medicine is the *only* one to use and rubbish the use of the medical profession. The kind of complementary medicines that I communicate about are such things as flower essences, gem elixirs, perfumed oils and spiritual healing in all its forms. There are also subjects such as reflexology, shiatsu, and massage. There are so many kinds of alternative medicine today and they each have their part to play in the role of healing. But they are not the total answer. They cannot for instance, heal a broken bone! Only a physician can do that with the proper tools and equipment. Complementary medicine can help to heal you quicker. It will also help to heal on the spiritual as well as the physical body.

I remember many Earth years ago, when my channel's daughter contracted a very rare disease called Sudeks Atrophy. Her daughter at 13 years of age had contracted a disease that was only prevalent in women of 80 or 90 years of age. My channel was distraught because the medical diagnosis was not good for her. She started to receive medical help, but we in the spiritual realms impressed upon my channel to try calcium tablets. Because the disease was of the bones we also suggested acupressure. With the combination of both the medical and complementary medicine, my channel's daughter was soon well and has had no occurrence since of the condition.

Proper diet, a happy life and contentment within, are all precursors of good health and continued good health. If an illness requires it, medical assistance should be sought from a medical professional. However, we do believe that as it is *your* body, you should be able to say what you do, or do not, ingest or take part in. If your intuition tells you that a certain medicine is not good for you, or that a certain treatment is not good, then you should be free to refuse that. So many souls do not speak up with regard to the medical profession. They hand over their power to a person often they have only just met or have known for only a short time. It is *your* body, *your* life, and *you* should dictate what happens to it. Do not be afraid to ask questions of your medical professional.

If you are ill, then seek out the help of complementary medicine, for this will help you on a spiritual level. You are more than the physical body. If only humankind would understand this, then there would be far fewer people with disease and illness on the Earth plane."

CONDITIONING

"Many times I hear people say, 'Oh, I have got rid of my conditioning,' and yet you have not. You see, conditioning is not just what has been forced into you by parents, friends and others, but it is also the subconscious belief systems as well.

All of your lives you have been fed a diet of what was right and what was wrong, very rarely have you been able to make decisions for yourself. This is called conditioning. It was fed to you from the moment that you were able to communicate and is probably *still* being fed to you in one way or another.

As you grew, you would have taken on much subconscious conditioning that you were not aware of, simply by listening subconsciously to those around you, especially your parents and guardians.

While I was out one day with my channel I was shocked to hear a woman call to her daughter in a most derogatory way. When her daughter did not answer her call, because she was in her own little world, the mother then called her 'Dumbo.' The child must have been called this many times because she instantly responded to the call. She will not realize the significance of such a name until she is older, and by then, the damage will have been done. The child is not aware that she is being ridiculed, and yet every time she is called that name (her real name is Lucy by the way) it goes into her subconscious mind.

Her mother was a very agitated woman. It is highly likely, that because she is around her mother a lot, absorbing in all her mother's energy, that she will also absorb her agitation. Yet she will not be aware of it because it is done on a subconscious level. It is possible for you to actually become your own mother, father, or guardian, because their thought system has become yours; their fear becomes yours, their negativity becomes yours.

Conditioning is deeply ingrained. It is created because souls cannot be, and often are not allowed to be their own person, make their own minds up and do their own thing. When you do this, and have the opportunity to do so, then you find a soul without conditioning and a soul who is truly in tune with the Universe.

It is wonderful to clear all conditioning from the soul, but what about all the subconscious fears, doubts, etc, that have been placed their subconsciously? It is *those* that you need to be aware of. When you become aware of them, then *you* truly become *your own person*."

CONFLICT

"For centuries of Earth time, the Middle East has been a place of conflict and war. The conflict and war has been over a small piece of Earth.

One side has said it belongs to them, another has said it is theirs by right. Yet nothing belongs to anyone! When you enter this world you come in with nothing, and when you leave, you leave with nothing. What you have in between is on loan for your learning and growth on this Earth plane. For those who fight over land, the fight has usually been going on for many Earth years. Each party fighting has their own belief system, their own illusion; each of them lives that illusion. They cannot see the futility of their actions; neither can they see that fighting for this piece of dirt will not change things.

The energy of ego, of the need to control started so long ago, is continuing to flow and destroy all those who come in contact with it. It is the very land they fight for that becomes their tormentor and jailer. So many places around the Earth are like this: Northern Ireland, the Middle East, Croatia, East Timor; the places are too numerous to mention. They do not understand that if they continue to fight they will still be fighting in another fifty Earth years. Yet neither party will share, because of religious beliefs, political beliefs or both. Can you not see that you are destroying yourselves? What does conflict do, it certainly does not heal!

I have said before that each man has his own truth. Why can humanity *not* have many truths? Only when mankind understands that each man can have his *own* truth, can war and conflict stop.

We who channel from the Spiritual realms have come to help you to see this. To hopefully educate humanity that you can all be different yet one nation, one world. When humanity does this, it will have truly raised its consciousness, and will finally find peace. Then all land will be shared, nobody will own anything. You never did anyway, you just thought you did. It is yours to use on your Earth plane journey."

CONSIDERATION FOR OTHERS

" Do you have consideration for others? Do you allow other people to make their mistakes and learn or grow, or, do you interfere, tell them they are doing the wrong thing and try and persuade them otherwise?

There is so much manipulation on the Earth plane today by souls who think they know best about another. Yet each soul has their own path, own vibration, own ideas, and an 'inner knowing' of what to do. If they follow this intuition, they will be led and guided every step of the way of their lives, to fulfil their destiny and fulfil their lives.

Humanity has such a habit of interference in others' lives; of feeling they know what is best for everyone. They do not! Only each soul knows what is best for itself.

Consideration for others means *not interfering* in another's life, belief system or faith.

It is hard seeing a fellow soul suffer; the heart cries out with wanting to help, but only through the pain and the suffering can one truly learn. Humanity says, "Why should we go through pain and suffering. Why would God want this?" God does not want it, nor does the energy of God choose it for you. It is *your* choice before you are born to choose the way, whether hard or easy, that you will grow and become a higher energy.

The Earth plane is the Hell that the Christians talk about, Heaven is the Spiritual.

It is here on the Earth plane that you can work through your karma, raise your vibration and become an enlightened being. *You* choose, as a soul, to come here. Your life mission, lessons and past mistakes can all be worked out here and can be found in your astrology chart. With this key you have the opportunity to move on; to become the enlightened being you would like to be.

The Earth plane also provides a *Self;* this is the Devil/Satan of the Christian faith. This energy, for it is an energy, is inside of you. It will do everything in its power to stop you moving forward. It is basically a battle between the Self and the Higher Self, which is the divine part of you. When you do *not* have consideration for others, you do not allow a soul to grow. In effect, you affect *their* life path by *your* decisions. Leave each soul to make their own."

CONTROL

"When you are in charge of your own life, the energy can flow to help you. Yet, too many of you still try to control not only your lives, but also the lives of others. Why do you do this? You do it because you are afraid to let go. You feel that you can be the other person. You do not realize that by controlling, or trying to control another, you take away their right to individual choice. In so many subtle ways, humanity feels the need to interfere in others lives. You each have individual choices. You each have your own destiny. When *another* lives that destiny for you, *you* stop the growth of your soul.

Even a child should be given the opportunity to make choices. It may not be *your* choice, but it is *their* choice. A child who makes choices in their life becomes more mature and can handle life a lot better than a child who is told what to do. A parent is there as a guide, to help the child in its path, he/she should not live the child's life for it. If they do this, they take away a basic freedom and stop spiritual growth. If a choice is made that could cause the child harm, this should be pointed out to the child. The child still has to learn, and through the experience of this will perhaps, learn a valuable lesson.

Husbands try to control wives; friends try to control friends. When each of you takes control of *your own* life and does not interfere in another's, each one of you can grow in spirituality and fulfil your own destiny without interference.

I am often asked, 'Master, why do I have to keep coming back in incarnation?' I say to these people, when you stop influencing another and stop interfering in others lives, then you will stop the process that keeps you coming back. It is as simple as that."

CRITICISM

"How many times a day do you criticize someone or something? Why do you do this? You do this because the person or issue you criticize acts as a mirror for you. The *Self*, seeing itself, does not want to see it. In retaliation it ridicules, makes fun of, criticizes, then it runs away.

There is a saying which I find quite interesting, 'All reaction is due to conditioning.'

You are conditioned to react to all that is not to your liking. It starts early; when children are at school and there is a situation to do with bullying, that *too* is a form of criticizing. One child, usually a sensitive child who is connected to the spiritual, even though they do not realize this is so, becomes a mirror for one other. This other one does not like what is presented to him through the mirror.

For instance, the child being bullied may be overweight, and the child seeing this looks into a mirror of their own weight problem, or subconscious fear of gaining weight. The one looking into the mirror then gets other children

37

to join in, or may do it alone. Then the bullying starts and they do not know why they do this. It could also be because of a past life remembrance. Remember that everyone who comes into your life is a mirror! Every soul has something to show or teach you. If you react, it is because you are not yet spiritually attuned.

With the one who is spiritually attuned and in vibration with their Higher Self, it is a waste of energy to react. They look in the mirror and they see the image, but they do not react. They do not give it energy. They either walk away from what they see with a desire to change it, or do not even see it, for their lives are involved in other things. The Self loves to react! Oh yes it does; it is the actor within each and every one of you. Some of them are great drama-queens, others are bit players, but you are all actors on a stage.

The next time that you find yourself reacting to something someone says, or does, or something that you see and do not like, just say to yourself, 'What a waste of energy reacting.' You will find that the energy will dissipate and you will have energy for other things. The more you react, the more you stay in the old way. Move forward and *don't react* and you will move into a higher vibration."

DEPRESSION

"What is depression? It is the body's way of dealing with change, buried emotion and stress. It is quite normal to be depressed, and when one is depressed one should try to ride it through. The human body is used to having one way of doing things. When change comes, it can create a huge turmoil in the physical. The same with buried emotions; the body has to cope as the emotion comes to the surface. Often there is a need to cry, but this is suppressed because it is not 'normal.'

The body has periods of Earth time when it is overloaded with stress. The person feels they are invincible and just keep pushing themselves. Then one day, they have to stop and the body goes into complete and utter chaos. This can also cause depression because the old way is not being followed; you are in a state of change but the body does not know how to cope.

When depression comes into your life do not fear it. It is there to make you look at your life and the way you are. Ask Spirit to help you find the answers. If you ask you will find them. Allow whatever is in there to come out, whether emotion (anger, frustration, fear, etc), stress, or just release. Do not fear it, for it is meant to help you cleanse away something that is no longer needed. If drugs are used to help the depression then seek the help of someone who can help you find the cause. You can also find natural sources to help you. It is nature's way of cleansing; remember that."

DIFFERENCES

"*ou* have your belief system. *You* have your own way of doing things according to your vibration and physical make-up. Why should others *not* have that same right?

39

Why does humanity insist on everyone being the same? It is because they do not understand the Spiritual within them. Yes, you all have a part of the Spiritual Soul within you, but many do not know, or are not aware of that part of themselves. The Creator, the Great Soul as many call him, God to others, created each one of you as a separate being. Even those of you who are twins or of multiple birth, have different personalities.

That personality part of you is the real you, the Spiritual within. You are *not* the same as your brother or any other human soul, you are unique! Think of that! You are the only one like you! The wonder of it, that the Creator, God, Divine Soul or whatever you call that energy, created *you* just as you, and then broke the mould so that nobody else could be like you. There are those of you who will say, 'But Master what about cloning, is that not making another of me?' and I will answer, 'Yes it will be a copy exactly of the physical you, but it cannot replicate your soul. That part of you is unique!'

If humanity is to leave behind war, hatred, fear, and all the other states of consciousness which for many Earth years have had control over their lives, they first of all have to understand, the differences between themselves and others. They have to understand that one can be a Moslem, one a Christian, yet they can still be friends and comrades. One a Jew, one an Orthodox Christian and still be friends and comrades. Just because they have a difference in their belief system should not be the cause of hatred or unhappiness.

Humanity has also to learn to love. So many souls do not know what it is to love or to receive love. It is the food that feeds the soul; without it you wither and die. Without it you are without a fundamental part of you. Humanity needs to learn of love if peace and happiness is to reign on the Earth plane. It starts with one soul accepting another, another's differences, another's belief system. When this is done, humanity can then build the bricks of a new society, one that has no differences, no concern over another's beliefs, and acceptance of *all* souls no matter what they choose to do. When this happens you will see anger, frustration and fear disappear; for it is the fear of another and their differences that is the cause of all problems on the Earth plane today.

I am here to teach *that* love; to help you find the Spiritual part of you, to help you free the soul. If you choose to listen, you will find change within yourself that will influence not only yourself, but also others. If you choose not to listen, you are not at this Earth time ready, but there will come a time when you are. For the vibration of the Earth plane is changing and bringing forth a new age; a time of renewal where all of the old will fall away and be replaced with new concepts and beliefs suitable for the time of the *Now*. How wonderful when that time comes!"

DIFFERENCES (II)

"ou are all different. Even twins are different; they may look the same, act the same, dress the same, but they are not the same. There are *no* two souls the same on the Earth plane. Just think of the souls who live there and then be aware of no two souls being the same. How incredible!

Each one of you is unique. Each one of you is a divine spark of God, attempting to get back to that energy. Each one of you will do it in your own way. You cannot do it the

41

same way as your friend or neighbour, because you are not the same as he/she. Neither can that soul do it like you. You are both different. You will however, do it in your own way.

It never ceases to amaze me how souls feel that other souls have to do it *their* way, when in fact they cannot, because they are not the same. When humanity can realize the differences in each other, when they can understand that there are many paths to God, what does it matter which path you take?

When they realize that each soul is a unique, being different to everyone else, then and only then will peace start returning to the Earth plane. The wars will stop and humanity will grow in Spirit. It *will* happen one day. In the meantime, understand your differences between yourself and others. Embrace their differences; do not condemn because someone does it different to you. This is how they choose to do it, their own way."

DISCERNMENT AND THE TRUTH

"In my teaching on Truth, I wrote about each man having his own truth. Each soul will find their own way of discerning the truth. They each have their own path astrologically. Some need to find truth, through finding the false, like my channel Margaret.

In the very early years of her development spiritually, she chose to go to a Healing Centre which left a lot to be desired in the way it was run. To Margaret, it seemed as if money was the motive, not the service. She chose not to return. Much later, when her Guardian Argos made his presence known to her, she asked him, 'why did you send me to that healing centre?' and the reply was, 'so that you would know *how not* to run a healing centre.'

Service must always be the motive if spiritual is to reside within. Other souls have to learn in other ways, but each soul will be led and guided to where and who they have to learn from. There are no accidents; all is perfect in the world. Often, souls who have had devastating experiences have said afterwards, 'I am glad I experienced that for I have grown because of it.' There are no *bad* experiences, only learning opportunities. Each soul chooses and is led, by us in the spiritual realms, to those that you need to learn from. Each soul will be led to their own truth."

DISCIPLINE & SPIRITUAL DEVELOPMENT

 "ou ask me, 'Master what can I do, to develop myself spiritually?' And I will answer, 'To become spiritually developed means to have discipline.'

You are *so* used to doing it your way when you feel like doing it. We also have our way, often it ties in astrologically with the planets.

So many souls ask to work for us. They say, 'Master please let us work for you!' So, we allow you to do so. But before long, you are complaining because you need time to yourself. To work for us, the Masters, means to give a total commitment. It does not mean to say that you hand over your freedom, you do not. But we are hard taskmasters, we have to be.

While working for us you are also working through the lessons you have to learn. Many souls think that because they work for us, they get concessions. This is not true. We *do* see that you *do not* need for anything, and we *do* open the doors for you, for opportunity to grow. However, you must earn the rewards and prove that you are worthy. There is a lot of hard work. Many souls do not last for very long.

Dedication, hard work and letting go of the Self, of one's own wants and needs, are the key points to passing through the spiritual tests. We do not set the test, *you do*, and we assist you to learn. When you ask for our help, it has already been pre-arranged before birth, but once we start to work with you and help discipline you, you run away, you cannot take the pace. It is not *my* will be done, but *thy* will be done. When one forgets about the Self, about one's own needs and desires, and begin to work with us, then spiritual growth starts to take place.

We can help you, but you have to do it *our* way. You have asked for this, because over many incarnations your way has not worked. The way of the Self has taken you down paths that stopped you from growing. Know that the path may be hard, it may be rocky, but at the end of the path is a rainbow and a peace that passeth all understanding. A peace one cannot describe. It is oneness with God and it is available to all those who surrender to us, who work with us and follow our promptings. We do not mean you to suffer. When you fight us, you will suffer. When you do not, everything will fall into place. It will be perfect if you do not fight. However, it is the path of the Self to fight, to hang in there until the bitter end.

All we do is show you how to by-pass the Self, how to work

with the Higher Self. It is not hard once you know how."

EMOTIONS

" have been asked on more than one occasion about emotions, what are they, and how do they affect our spiritual lives? First of all, I must emphasize that when I am writing about emotions, I am referring to negative emotions such as anger, etc. The emotional body is a part of humanity tied to the animal part of you. It is a part of the *Self,* a separate body which is designed to hold you back from moving forward. It knows all your fear, anger, frustration, weak and negative parts of you, and it is capable of pulling itself out of a hat, like magic, whenever it needs to slow you down.

I was asked once about happiness, 'Is not happiness an emotion?' and I say not. I say that happiness is a feeling. It is not happiness that holds you back. It is not happiness that stops you from growing. It is happiness which urges you on. It is a positive not a negative energy.

I hope that for some souls, this will answer a question they have had for some time. It is only the negative emotions which the Self clings to, uses and abuses. That is the difference."

ENEMIES

" ften, your enemies on the Earth plane can be your friends from the realms of the spiritual world, who have come to help you to learn lessons. Instead of hating these people, love them, because

45

they give you the greatest opportunity to grow and be free of your karma.

So many souls have hate in their hearts because people have hurt them or upset them. Often, that hate will never be dealt with and will be taken, incarnation after incarnation, until in one incarnation it will manifest as illness. Every soul who comes into your life, comes to teach you something. The person may be your mother or father, family member or someone close, but no matter what they did, they did it to help you. Instead of feeling hate, turn that hate into love; thank the person for being there to help you. Often, the person who becomes your enemy, the person you come to hate or despise, is your best friend in the spiritual realms chosen by you to help you to grow. They have agreed to be a part of your life to do this.

When you can let go of your hate for all those who have hurt you, and replace this with thanks and love for the opportunities they have given you to grow and learn, then you become such a great soul. Let go of your anger, hatred, bad feelings and be thankful that someone cared enough to help you. That in itself is true friendship."

ENERGY

"uch has been written about the payment of money for spiritual favours. There have been many who think that because it is of God, then it must be given freely; that those who charge a fee for their services are, 'greedy and not spiritual.'

You have a saying on your Earth plane, 'God helps those

who help themselves.' If you provide a service and you share your energy, then, if that energy is given away, it is worth nothing. A labourer is worthy of his hire. Many experienced spiritual teachers have studied for many years, sacrificed much, and worked often without an income to learn their profession. What do they use for energy if they do not charge a fee? How do they pay their airfares to attend workshops and teachings, their hotel accommodation and expenses? How do they pay for their home, the food on the table and the clothes they wear? How do they provide for their families?

One should always tithe (share) what one receives with those less fortunate than oneself. Many people do this with their income. If you tithe to those less fortunate, then you open up the energy to receive more. If one receives an income then this is energy, and if energy is constantly in motion, then it does not stop.

Perhaps you could liken material energy, whether it be money or material items, to a house with electricity. When the energy is flowing around the house then the house is lit up and the energy is flowing. When the energy is switched off, it is stagnant, waiting to start up again, and the house is in darkness. When you stop the flow of energy because you worry, doubt, fear or have any other negative emotion, then you switch off the power in the house. When you allow the energy to flow, then it stays constant.

There is always a reason why people want more, why they hang on so tightly to their possessions and material things. What is your reason? What is your fear? Is it from a past life, or in this life? Find the reason, and you will find the answer to abundance without end; a constant flow without end.

47

You hoard your material possessions, you fear change, you hang on to people, and you hang on to your energy not realizing that you stop the flow. Let the energy flow. Be not afraid and allow abundance into your life."

EUTHANASIA

"There has been much controversy in recent years on the subject of euthanasia – the taking of one's own life to end years of pain and suffering. This is indeed a controversial subject. I would like to express the views of we in the spiritual realms on this subject.

Each soul, before it is born, chooses its life span and circumstances. When you are doing this, we ask you, 'Do you think this situation could be too hard for you?' Most often the response is, 'No.'

When you come to the Earth plane to begin your incarnation, it is only when you are enduring the situations you have chosen, that sometimes, it seems too much and you feel you have to return home. You may think your life is finished then, but it is not. Say for instance, you have chosen to live a life of 85 years, and you return home by your own hand (suicide) at the age of 70 years. Of your outstanding contract you chose before you were born, you still have 15 Earth years of experience left. You will have to return to the Earth plane for that 15 years remaining. You will then return home and your contract is closed. *You* choose your circumstances, country of birth, parents, etc, we do nothing except advise you. *You* are the creator of every incarnation you have.

If you have ever wondered why souls come to the Earth plane and only live a short time, sometimes only days, it is because they are finishing off a past life experience. When that life experience is finished, they then return home.

You make the choice of whether you stay or return home. You, as I stated earlier, are the creator of your own reality. *You are not punished because you choose to return home early!* However, if for instance you chose to have cancer and die from this disease, by taking your life early, you will return to the Earth plane for your time remaining. You still have to live the contract. However, just the people, who are helping you experience this are changed, and perhaps the location. The lessons you have chosen and not fulfilled, still remain. Nobody should make comment because of *your* choice.

Each one of you is born with free will, and can at any time exercise that free will. They do not have *your* pain, *your* lack of a reasonable standard of life. How can they know how you feel? Often when you do return early, we will point out to you that we did tell you this part of your life would be hard, but that is all we do and we certainly do not judge you. After a short rest, then you return to finish that contract.

For those reading this who disagree with this, perhaps one day, you too will have cancer or a disease which causes great pain. Only then, will you be able to understand the life of one who has chosen this as their life lessons. The Christian Bible states, 'Judge not, lest ye be judged also.' Do not judge anyone, this is *their* choice!"

EVERYONE
HAS A HEART

"Everyone has a heart; they just have to learn how to use it. The heart is the most important part of humanity. It is where love is created, stored and used.

When the heart is full of anger, resentment, fear, doubt, insecurity, it is closed. It cannot radiate the love from the Universe, the love from God, the Ultimate Being. When the heart is closed, not only can it *not* radiate love, it *cannot* feel love. It is as if a barrier is there, stopping the love from entering.

Many spiritual people profess to a have an open-heart chakra. Yet they, more than anything, are usually the ones that have them closed. They speak ill of others, preach negative words and have fear in their hearts. Note that I said many, not all! There are many spiritual souls with beautiful hearts and minds. Their principal concern is love and nothing else but to serve humanity in love.

If the Earth plane is to change, it cannot change with people preaching! It has to come from learning how to use the heart; the very source of the soul and of the love from God, the Ultimate Being. Each soul is entitled to this love. It is available for all but only a few can experience it. When they *do* learn, they will experience a bliss and peace beyond understanding."

EXCESS BAGGAGE

" **I** have written often of past life energy that you are carrying around with you, and the energy of this incarnation. But many of you also carry around with you, like excess baggage, the emotions and feelings of others which you have absorbed, and been exposed to, during your life.

Often, the energy is not your own but that of others. As you experience life, so many of you absorb the thought forms of others, simply by being in their energy. Children often absorb the energy of their siblings or parents, not realizing that they are doing so. Later in life, during crisis or healing, this can often come to the surface. You are not only a sum total of your own past and present, but you can also be carrying around the energy of others. When you become aware of this, then one can work with the energy and release it."

FAMILY

" **I** f one is to have peace in the world, then one has to start with one's own family.

So much dissension is caused in families because parents seem to think that they have full, or partial, control over their family members. Whether it be a daughter, who disapproves of her mother or father marrying again; or a parent, who disapproves of their daughter's choice of husband or the way they live their life. Discord in families

51

is a major problem in the world today.

My channel has a daughter who is a very lovely soul. She has chosen to come to the Earth plane and work out her karma, and hopefully grow as a soul. Although my channel gave her daughter a wonderful education and everything in the home that she could want (she wanted for nothing), that is where the problem started. She tended to spoil and smother her daughter, because her previous daughter was given away for adoption before marriage, so this one was very precious to her.

Although the daughter was taught spiritual values, when she was sixteen years of age, this young woman decided that she wanted her freedom, and so, she left home to walk in uncharted waters and to live life for herself. My channel was hurt, devastated, and for a while tried to control her from a distance through gifts of food and other personal items. But eventually the daughter ran right away and for a number of years did not see her mother.

During this time, we in the spiritual realms, very gently enabled my channel to see that *she* had created part of the problem with her daughter; that her daughter was *only* a soul who had passed through her womb on a long journey back to spiritual realms. When my channel realized this, the pain started to subside. She looked at her daughter through different eyes, finally letting go of her and allowing her to be her own person. Since that time, the daughter has got herself into quite a bit of trouble. She has learned a lot about people, life in general and about survival, and is still doing so. My channel does not condemn her daughter; and because she was able to forgive and realize that her daughter was *not* her possession to own, but a soul in its own right, gradually, they have been reconciled.

There is writing by a man called Kahlil Gibran, who many call, 'The Prophet.' He was a very intuitive man and a channeller, and wrote on many different subjects. He says, *'Your children are not your children. They are the result of life's longing for itself. They come through you, not from you!'* And this, in a simple way, is what life is all about.

Many people on Earth today have altercations with family members because they want to hold them to themselves. They are so insecure that they fear the person will leave them and never return. That fear then becomes a reality. What they fear, what they think, they create. For everything in the Universe there is an equal and opposite force. What you try to hold on to will be pulled away from you. What you allow to be free will return.

It is not easy having family members, who according to *your* belief system do the wrong thing. But how do *you* know that they do the wrong thing? Are you Judge and Jury? Only the Creator, the Divine Soul can do that. You are not in a position to judge, for you could have made the same mistake in a past life or may do, in the future.

If your children, parents or family members chose to do things different to you, that is their choice. I am often asked, 'What stage should I let go of my children?' And I say to them, when they are old enough to make decisions for themselves. This can be ten years of age or sixteen years of age or five years of age. Remember that your children are not your possession, neither are your parents or other family members. They have chosen you to help them to learn lessons. Those lessons can be good, or bad,

53

according to what the person has chosen. But often, your opinions are not in accordance with them and this is where problems begin.

I have heard many souls say, 'Because you are marrying that person I will never speak to you again.' How do you know that the person they are marrying is not in their life to teach them lessons? *Your opinion* can often stop a soul from growing or learning their lessons.

If you have dissension in your family because of a child, parent or family member going against your belief system, or doing something you disapprove of, then understand that they chose to do so as part of their learning. And that by doing so they will grow and perhaps never have to return to incarnate again. If you stop them, you create the possibility of another incarnation for them. What a responsibility for yourself!

Until there is family happiness, there will never be peace on Earth. When my channel knew that she was going to be channelling my teaching on family she said, 'Master what if people find out about my wayward daughter and persecute or judge me for the way she is?' I said to her, your child is not wayward, she is just strong and determined. She has chosen a hard road in this incarnation, but one that will teach her many things. If people judge you because of her, that is *their* problem, it is not yours. You gave her the life she has. You provided the womb and a safe environment until she chose to leave. Do not chastise yourself for the failings that you assume your daughter has. She is on her path like all the other souls on this Earth plane.

Peace will only come when families learn to love unconditionally, and learn to let go of their anger and hatred towards family members who do not conform to their ideas.

Love can then enter and bring with it, joy, happiness, reconciliation and peace."

FEAR

"Why do you have fear? What is fear? Fear is when you know or feel you cannot do something. Although fear is a surface emotion, the cause of it is always connected to two reasons. One reason is because you have had the experience before in a past incarnation and you did not react to it in a positive way. Secondly, you do not feel you are capable of doing it. You do not feel good or worthy enough.

Fear is the *Self* in all its glory. The Devil and Satan of the Christian religion is one aspect of it. Yet what is fear? When one looks at fear, *not* as fear, but as energy, it becomes a totally different thing. To progress spiritually, one can have no fear, for fear creates blocks and negative conditioning in the auric field. This then repels any positive energy coming towards you. You can say to the Universe, I need a certain thing, but if you have a fear of attaining it and having it, you will stop the flow immediately. So many of you have subconscious fears also, and do not even realize you have them.

Once you face your fear it ceases to be. It is gone. Yet, while you have the fear you are rigid at even the thought of it. That rigidity will bind you in a prison forever, unless you become more pliable. What is your fear? Where does this fear come from? You may say, 'It comes from an experience in this life,' and yet, you will usually find it is connected to past lives too. Only by going into that lifetime and freeing yourself from it, will you be free of the fear. You may say, 'I do not think I am good enough, capable enough, strong enough, etc, to do it,' and while you make that statement you *never* will be.

I am often asked, 'Master what can I do to help myself spiritually?' And I say to the person, "Look at your fears, what they are, where they are. Make a list of them. One by one work through them, and as you do so, you will become stronger. You will clear blocks that have often been there for many lifetimes, and then, you *will* progress spiritually."

FREEING THE SOUL FROM FEAR

"I am often asked, 'Master, what do I have to do to free my soul from the wheel of incarnation?' This is not a difficult thing to do. It is achieved by facing your fears and doubts. By learning to have faith and trust in the spiritual world. By not wanting to do it *your* way, but by *waiting* on the spiritual world to lead you and guide you. By going within, either on your own or with the help of an experienced therapist, to find what is hiding in your soul from past lives. By letting go of established conditioning, either from your parents or again from past life experiences, which are still in the soul.

Each time you clear away one of these issues, you leave a

bigger space for the spiritual realms to enter. The more space, the more spiritual helpers can work with you and for you. Eventually there are no blocks, just space; then the soul can leave unhindered, never to return into incarnation. There is no easy way out. No short cut. It takes hard work and effort. It can be achieved. Then the soul is free.

Why not start the process of Ascension now?"

GOD DOES NOT WANT US TO SUFFER

"On my travels I have often been asked, 'Master, why does God make us suffer?' I reply, 'God does not make you suffer, you create that situation yourselves.'

Whether you know God as the Creator, Mother Father God or Divine Soul, this energy is with you, all around you, and all embracing. It would never want to hurt you because it loves you unconditionally. It does not care what religious faith you are, what colour skin you have, how much spirituality you have, this energy loves you as you are."

You can say, 'but I am a Christian,' and I will say, 'but this energy loves you.' Or you may say, 'but Master, I am a Jew,' and I will repeat my previous statement. Or you may say, 'but Master I am not spiritual,' or, 'I have been to prison,' or, 'I have been a bad person,' and I will say to all and everything, 'but you are loved by God, or whatever name you give this Energy. It is *you* who does not love yourself!'

57

This Energy wishes to help *all* of you. But until you can

learn to love yourself, it cannot; because what this energy builds up inside of you, your low self-esteem, lack of confidence and lack of love for yourself, will destroy. You can say, 'Master, how can I love myself?' and I will say to you, 'by forgiving yourself for anything you have accused yourself of.'

Often you will be asked to help the spiritual realms and will refuse this task, but God will still love you because life is made up of choices and *you* make the choices.

How many times have you persecuted yourself because of your imperfections? God does not persecute. God accepts you as you are. It makes no demands.

When you can start learning to love yourself, then God, under whatever name you call this Energy, can do the work of loving you unconditionally. Until you can love yourself, your negative feelings about yourself will block that love. You have never done anything wrong, you have just taken the wrong road, made the wrong choice, or misused energy. Life is a continual learning experience. If you did not make mistakes as you on Earth call it, you would never learn. There are no mistakes, only choices.

Forgive yourselves for anything you have persecuted yourself for and open up to unconditional love!"

HAPPINESS

"Happiness is the right of every soul, yet so many of you on the Earth plane are unhappy and miserable. Why is this so? It is because you do not know where your happiness is. Many of you have never looked within yourselves to see what it is that you can be happy doing. You do not believe that you are capable of being happy in anything. Negativity weighs around you like dead weights, and the unhappier you are the more the weight.

Each one of you has talents, something that you can do to make a living for yourself, and also, to make life enjoyable for yourselves. Once you discover your talent then you want to go to work. You want to get out of bed in a morning. You enjoy every day. You want less sleep and every day becomes a joyous occasion. You have a constant smile on your face and your energy is boundless.

It takes courage to find your talent, because once you do find it, then you have to apply it and that can bring change. The Self hates change, and will avoid it wherever it can. You can say, 'but Master how do I find out what my talents are?' and I will say to you, 'it is what you are good at best of all.' Some people are good in a creative way, others in communication, others spiritual, others with logic. Every soul has their talent, find it and you can find your happiness. If you want to take the easy way to finding your talent then you can find a spiritual teacher/reader, one who works on a spiritual level and they will channel the information about your talent.

Do *not* be unhappy any more, set yourself free and find the happiness that is meant to be for you. Do not fear change, it brings with it wonderful opportunities to change your life forever. Do not let your age stop you either; many souls have changed direction late in life and made a better life for themselves. If you are an unhappy soul then find your talent and find happiness."

59

HEAVEN on EARTH

"We cannot do our work on the physical plane without your help. For many years of Earth time, humanity has been bound by the Self. The time has come when humanity has decided to change. Many souls offered themselves as, what many would term 'light workers' before their incarnation on the Earth plane. The time has come when we are ready to assist humanity with the change and with the higher consciousness. However, when we need your help, many souls are running away. The Self is taking control. It is our intention to bring Heaven to Earth. In other words, if change takes place in humanity, it will be possible for all on the Earth plane to experience the joy, peace and balance of, what some would term, Heaven on the Earth plane.

We can assist you to do that. However, when we ask for your help, we need you to be there. Many of you, in the past few Earth years, have felt the calling to work with us but have either stalled doing so, or run away. We have sent teachers to help you, but you have seen these teachers as fearful people, when in fact they are mirrors for you; showing you what you do not want to see in yourselves. The measure of a good teacher is what they show you that you do not want to see in yourself.

In the next twelve Earth years, we will need many to help us, if we are to do the work of bringing Heaven to Earth. What we have in the spiritual planes, you can have on Earth. We cannot do this alone though; it takes *you* on the

Earth plane to assist us in the physical form. If you feel the calling, then ask to be led to one who can help you. Then allow *nothing* to get in your way. You call out to us, 'Masters, we wish to change the Earth plane,' but when we say, 'we have heard you, we are on our way,' you run or are enveloped in fear. We do not want to harm or hurt anyone, just to show you a better way of life, an easier way of life.

Please let us help."

HOW CAN I SERVE HUMANITY?

" am often asked, 'How can I serve humanity? How can I help the world?'

You can do this by stepping out of the Self. Stepping out of the fear of your life and giving of yourself to help others.

It does not matter how you give, whether teaching, healing or working in other areas. All that matters is that you step outside of the Self and allow the energy of the Universe to lead and guide you to your path. It can happen. All you need to do is to trust and to believe that Spirit will assist you. We are just waiting for you to have complete faith in us!

Your Self will have you imagine that we will hurt you or control you, but all we wish to do is to assist you to grow and learn; work with you to assist humanity and lead and guide you to a better life. We will help you if you will help yourself; your Higher Self that is. Your Higher Self has all the answers. Your Higher Self knows your path, your destiny, and can lead you through the minefield of life in a far easier way than the Self can.

Your Self will destroy you if it can for it does not want to leave the comfort zone. Your Higher Self only wishes to educate you and take you to a higher vibration. Once you can do this, then you can serve humanity. For the Self will do everything it can to stop you. It will bring out all the fear, doubt, disbelief, and this will stop you in your tracks. However, if you fight the fear, have the belief, have no doubt, and *believe* in a higher source of energy, then your life will change. It will change so much that you will bring all that you desire into your life.

There is nothing wrong in having abundance in your life, in having money and success. It is what you do with it that is important. If it is used to help humanity on its path, then it is truly being used for good. How can you serve humanity if you are poor? Yes, I can see your Self finding an answer for this question. Yet, without funds or material assets, one can be limited and frustrated if one wishes to help in certain ways. You limit yourselves in so many ways. However, once *you believe* that abundance is yours and it can be used to help others, then it will surely come into your life.

Often there can be a past life residue from a convent, monastery or a poverty type existence that is behind the lack. If you have a poverty consciousness and wonder where this comes from, then find the answer through past life regression and remove it from your energy. Then you can use the abundance to assist humanity."

HOW TO BE TRULY SPIRITUAL

"One cannot be truly spiritual if one has one grain of anger, fear, doubt, envy and other emotions. Yes, one can say, 'I am spiritual,' but if you have any negative thinking to another soul, or a situation, then you cannot be truly spiritual in the true sense of the word. How many of you react to situations that you know you should not react to? How can the world be healed, if individual souls cannot heal themselves. It is *within* the personal (person) that one needs to start changing the negative within one. How many of you have problems with your brother, sister, mother, father, friend or work associate? Yes, I am speaking to *you* who answered that statement. How can the world be changed until peace is found within? How often do you find yourself justifying yourself? How often do you find yourself becoming angry with someone? What a waste of energy! Just think what you could do with that wasted energy! You could manifest something you desire or educate yourself. There are so many ways to use the energy in a positive way. The more you do this, the more you will be able to create and manifest. It just takes *you* to stop the flow of negative energy.

I can hear you saying now, 'but the person will not speak to me,' and I will reply, 'do you need them in your life – truly need them in your life?' You are here for your own life, not for anyone else's! If you can stand in front of God, as you know this Energy, and *know* that you are without blemish, that is all that matters. Your justifying yourself to someone does not change things because there will always be two points of view. As I wrote in another message, 'Each man has his own truth.'

Why is it important that *you* are right? Do you think you will lose face by not justifying yourself? I will tell you, you will not! You will move forward in consciousness because you will no longer be trapped in the old energy of justification. You will no longer be living in a stagnant energy.

As you let go, as you move forward, you will then begin to see a new side of life, one you could not see before because you were caught in conflict.

Let go of the need to be right, to be the victor. Do not give anything any energy. What does it matter, except to the Self, *who* has to do this? Because this is what it thinks it must do, because of habit over years of a lifetime. Just walk away! Let it become the other person's problem not yours. Give it no energy at all. You will soon see a difference in your life. Yes, there will be the sadness of letting go, perhaps the situation has been happening over many incarnations. However, one soon heals, just remember that. The healing process starts immediately you let go!"

HOW WE COMMUNICATE WITH YOU

" am often asked how communication can occur between the spiritual world and the soul. This is surprisingly, not hard to do. For the majority of your life, the Self, which is the Mind, is constantly on alert. It is your protector and never stops working in looking after you. It does not like change. If change occurs it will bring up all of your fears, doubts, insecurities, all of the negative emotions, to stop you from making change. Your *Self* knows you better than you know yourself!

You also have a Higher Self; this part of you is connected to the spiritual part of you. It is like a telephone line between you and us in the spiritual realms. However, imagine the telephone line having a huge boulder on it stopping communication. This is what it is like when the Self is the controlling force. In order for us to communicate with you, we first of all need the Self to be occupied. It may surprise many that my channel Margaret does not meditate, she never has. There has always been a communication line open, despite her Self, between she and I. In the last few Earth years we have become one, as she has freed herself of the Self's control.

In the early days of her development we would communicate with her when the Self was occupied. This would be when she was doing her household chores. When she was ironing or cooking or cleaning. The Self was occupied in mundane tasks, very unaware of our presence. At this time, we could then communicate with her through the Higher Self. She was born with the knowledge that she had to ask us to communicate with her, and this is very important to know. *We need to know that you wish to communicate with us!* When the Self, which is the Mind, is occupied, then we can communicate on another level. We can send inspiration to you, give you information to help you on your life path and send wonderful healing energy to you.

There are many who believe that it is imperative to meditate, that only true communication with spiritual realms can take place when this is happening. Many souls can meditate and enjoy doing so; for them, it is the highlight of their day to sit and communicate with us. For others it becomes a struggle and a frustration and this should not be so.

You cannot, however, communicate with us while you are worried and anxious; racing around doing a hundred and one things. That will definitely not work. We need you to be relatively still, doing gardening, housework, menial or necessary work. You need to be occupied. Even reading a book can enable us to communicate. Tell us that you wish to communicate. You can call upon us as God, Divine Soul, Masters, whatever you wish to call us and you feel comfortable with.

For many years of Earth time Margaret, my channel, would call out when she was occupied, 'Hey you upstairs!' It did not worry us; we knew then, that she was ready to receive our information. She received many, many communications when she was doing her ironing.

It is simply a matter of having the Self occupied and allowing us to then communicate through the Higher Self. It is also important that you take heed of the messages coming through. Listen to the intuition and allow it to be.

Communicating with spiritual realms and learning to let go of the Self can take a period of Earth time before it is perfected. For some it will take time before they do communicate. For others, it will be instantaneous.

This does not mean that you can stop working at clearing the Self, that work must go on, but you will find that the more you can allow the Higher Self access, the stronger it will become. When the Self is occupied it is not aware of anything but its allotted task. It is ignorant of the Higher Self and what is happening on that level.

The secret to communication with us is to ask for our help. When you ask, you will receive. Does not one of your holy books contain this saying?

There will be many souls who will say that they are not worthy of spiritual communication. Margaret, my channel, felt this way for many years because she had such a low opinion of herself. Of course, she is no longer that way; we enabled her to change that. Our teachings helped her plus her own work that she did on herself. But I will tell you that *no* soul is turned away. You are all special to us and we want to help you. You have to be willing to meet us half way.

Try it and see what happens. If it works for you, please communicate to others about this. I know that there will be many souls who will be able to receive help."

INDEPENDENCE

"It is time that humankind learned that each one of them can make themselves independent, from anyone or anything, and that by doing so, they can also raise their vibration spiritually.

Each soul who arrives on the Earth plane for an incarnation has a talent, and an ability to use that talent for their own advancement and prosperity. Many souls however, are not aware of that talent, and spend a lot of time being dependent on government help financially. No

67

soul should have to depend on a handout for their living. No soul should have to sleep in a cardboard box or in the streets under rags. Each soul has within them, the talent to create a wonderful and secure financial future for themselves, if only they knew how.

Society on Earth has created a situation where those who are working, through their taxes, pay for the income of those who don't. Those who don't have an income sink lower and lower in self-esteem and get caught in the spider's web which is provided by the government. That provision is usually minimal, designed to give the bare essentials financially. Families and individuals who take the opportunity to live that way, usually find it very difficult to escape once they take part, and so a pattern is set.

Each soul is worth something, and each soul has talent of some sort. There is never a soul who does not come with talent. It is difficult however, to find that talent in an education system that only encourages academics. There are many souls who are not academic, and yet they are made to feel inferior because they are not. They leave school feeling they are losers, no hopers, and have no future. Every soul has a future, every soul has a talent, and once that talent is found, they can then open a whole new door for themselves.

The use of intuition is not encouraged, and yet it can be the biggest help to souls in finding their path and their talent. There are no spiritual people in the education system to help the souls tune into their Akashic record and find their purpose in life. Years ago, the Shaman, or wise man or woman, or the priest or priestess of the village would do this.

Spirituality is not about forcing one to believe in God, nor in being holy or religious, it is about being at one with the Divine Soul, and allowing those who do have the gifts of the spiritual realms, seers, diviners, spiritual clairvoyants to guide one to one's destiny, to show the way to one's talent and one's future. Oh, if only this were so, there would be no souls living on government handouts.

While the government provides a living for people, the souls will take what is provided. When a government forces one to use one's own talent by not providing assistance, then a soul can achieve their destiny. Find your talent, and you will find your destiny. When you find your destiny, you will find happiness and will, if you allow yourselves, move towards that destiny and start a new life for yourselves. You will no longer then be dependent on another for your income."

INTUITION

"Every soul on the Earth plane has intuition. There are also some souls who have a heightened intuition. These souls have usually had many previous lives where the intuition has been used. In this incarnation it is very close to the surface. It is to these souls that we in Spirit speak.

Some of you have been awaiting the call to work with us, others chose to do this in this incarnation. We work through your intuition, your sixth sense. For some it is very easy to open up to Spirit, for others this takes considerable Earth time.

If you will listen to your inner voice you will know whether

69

you have chosen to connect with us. It will be an inner knowing, a feeling that it is to be. It will be felt very strongly within your heart.

If you wish to work with us, then tell the Ultimate Being, or as you know this energy, God. The process will then start to enable us to work with you.

Communion with you is a slow process, do not expect it to be quick. Much has to change within the physical body to enable us to blend with you.

Listen to your intuition, never doubt it, for it is the connection from you to us."

JUDGEMENT

o many of you on the Earth plane today have a tendency to judge others. When one judges another, one judges oneself. It is the Self who judges. Why do you have to do this? Each one of you is a unique individual with your own lessons to learn; everything is perfect in the universe and if this is so, then all is happening as it should. When one makes judgment, one becomes judge and jury. Yet there is only one judge and that is the Supreme Being or God, as many of you know this energy, the Great Akashic, where all debts are stored. If you judge another you become worse than the one you judge, because you break a great Universal Law.

When one makes a judgment against another, one is saying *you* did this wrong, and yet how do you know that they did this wrong? Are *you* God or the Supreme Being? At the same time, you hold yourself back spiritually so much by that judgment. Just because you *think* or *feel* it is wrong is not an excuse. Nobody has the right to judge another.

Each one of you on this Earth plane, at some time or other, has judged another. Why do you do this? It is the Self who does this. The Higher Self would never do this because the Higher Self is connected to the Supreme Being, God. It knows that all men have their own path and their own reasons for doing things.

The saying in your Christian Bible, 'Judgment is mine, sayeth the Lord,' is so true. Only the Supreme Being, God, has that ability to judge, and when it has looked at the situation, it then marks the Akashic. Many times I have heard many of you say, 'There but for the grace of God go I.' All of you at some time in your existence, through your many incarnations, have done exactly what you are doing now, you judge.

Do not judge another, either for personal reasons or for business. By doing this you lay so much karma at your feet."

KARMA

"You often cry out in your pain and suffering, 'God why is this happening to me? I am a good person, why am I suffering?' The reason for this and for all life purpose is karma. It is the repayment of debts and the receiving of debts.

From the minute of Earth time that you are born you begin the path to repaying your karma, receiving karma, and to clearing your Akashic record. If you can do it in this incarnation, then you free yourself from the wheel of life. Look at a mouse in a cage pushing the wheel! That is you on your wheel of life. Constantly pushing, moving forward, but never getting there. Occasionally you may get off and have a rest, and then get back on again, but until you can clear your Akashic and control all of the subtle bodies, physical, mental, emotional and spiritual, then you are in the cage on the continual wheel, incarnation after incarnation.

There are many spiritual people today who have beautiful spiritual gifts, and are wonderful healers or light workers for us in the spiritual world, but they still have not controlled one or more of their subtle bodies. Until they do this they cannot move forward to the higher level.

How do you control the subtle bodies? Let us start at the beginning with the physical body. The desires of the physical must be controlled, for balance must be attained in all the subtle bodies. Desires for food, excessive compulsions, any desires of the flesh must be controlled if one is to control the physical body. For each subtle body has a Self and a Higher Self and one must attain the Higher Self in everything.

In the mental body, one must learn to control one's thoughts, all thoughts. If one has a negative thought about anything, then one cannot be in control of the mental body. Remember that it is *thought* that creates what you think. You will create as you raise your vibration higher, so control of the mental body is most important.

Controlling the emotional body is the next step, not allowing your emotional body to be out of control. Many of you on this Earth plane take what is said to you in a personal manner and get upset over trivial matters. This creates a blockage in the heart chakra and an unbalance in the emotional body.

Finally there is the control of the spiritual body. Learning to use this body wisely, using the sixth sense, the psychic, and the universal energy in a right and proper manner. When you have done this, then you can communicate with the Higher Source and know the peace that passeth all understanding.

The path to controlling the Self in each subtle body is a long and arduous task. It will not happen overnight and will take at the least, ten to fifteen years of Earth time from when you start your path of learning. All kind of tests are thrown in your way. The purpose of all incarnations is to free you of the limitations you have placed in your subtle bodies. However, once you reach the Earth plane and take incarnation, the Self takes control again and the battle between the Self and the Higher Self begins. Many incarnations go by before the control of the subtle bodies is achieved. Sometimes souls plead for help in freeing themselves of their limitations and ask the Lords of Karma for assistance, and then a teacher or a healer is found to help them, and arrangements made to work with them in an incarnation.

For many souls on the Earth plane at this time, opportunities await them to learn to free themselves of the subtle body limitations. The Photon Belt energy, the Christ Soul, is the energy enabling mankind to free themselves of limitation.

As there is the power of light, there is also the power of darkness. The darkness is the Self of all your subtle

73

bodies. It does not want to let go so it will create fear, illusion, doubt, insecurity and lack of confidence. It will hold you back because it does not want to let go – why should it, it has had free rein for many thousands of incarnations. Illusion is the worst thing that the Self will create. It can create a situation that has you believing something that is totally untrue.

The Higher Self though, knows the truth. It has no negative thoughts and feelings. It just *is*. It is the *I am* of all. When union with the Higher Self is achieved then total peace is assured. There are many who think they have achieved the controlling of the subtle bodies, who feel that they have everything in control, but only by their actions will you know if this is so. If they criticize another, if they doubt, have fear, judge another, allow anything negative in their life then they have not done this. Even one small criticism of another is enough to stop this.

For those who have learned to control the subtle bodies and have passed the tests placed in front of them, the light shines from their bodies. They are in control of all that they do. The love for their fellow humans shines forth from their heart chakra and they are truly of man and God. When this is done, then can the Earth plane be left behind once and for all."

KILLING

"What makes humanity kill? One of the main culprits is anger in humanity. People think they are calm, yet in sixty percent of the population of the Earth, subconscious anger, rage and frustration lies within the soul. It is hidden and does not manifest itself unless it is triggered. The person, throughout their lives, holds in all of their frustration. They do not let go of their anger. It stays inside, accumulating, waiting for the cork to be pulled either in this incarnation or in another.

Do you know there would be no anger in the world if humanity learned to communicate with each other without argument, jealousy, fear, or other negative emotions? This is true. If humanity were to learn how to communicate with each soul without negative feelings, there would be no anger.

People or situations that come from past life experiences can often trigger anger! Let me explain. Let us have a scenario. In another incarnation two people had problems communicating. One became very angry and did not release that anger. Once this person returned to the spiritual realms they would have seen what they did wrong, and would then attempt to right that wrong. They would incarnate again to let go of the anger. The same person who provoked them could decide to return also and 'trigger' the release of the anger. The two meet in this incarnation. When they meet, one of them dislikes the other, the one with the anger feels it rising again. They do not understand why this is happening and they part, still

75

not liking and trusting each other. However, the 'trigger' has been released and in a short Earth time, the anger is released in a safe way.

Another scenario is that people find themselves in exactly the same situation as they were before and the soul memory of this triggers the release of the anger.

Only when humanity learns to be at peace with one another, will peace reign on Earth. You are all like mice on a wheel, going round and round and round, incarnation after incarnation, repeating the same feelings, emotions and anger. Only when you become aware of this, will you stop the killing."

LESSONS

"Each one of you is a soul, who is a student in a school! Your friends, lovers, partners and family are the teachers in this school. Each Earth day, they mirror for you what you *do not* want to see in yourself. They come into your life to teach you valuable life lessons, or just to mirror for you, what you do not wish to see within yourself. If you took the time to understand this, your life would be so much easier.

Each of you has old stale energy in the subconscious, which you have come to free yourself of. It is the job of the Self to hold onto this as long as it can, maybe not letting go at all. The people around you, who mirror for you, are there to help you to confront these issues. However, the usual reaction when faced with these phenomena is to run away! It is the fear of letting go of it. The Self will give you a thousand reasons why you should run, and it is very good in its persuasion. How many times have you run away because you did not like what someone said or did, or just their energy? Many times I am sure. The school of life is not easy, it is not meant to be. One cannot learn while one is in the comfort zone of life.

The next time you are faced with something you do not like, in someone or something, see it through, don't run away. You will be surprised how you handle this. Yes, there could be fear, but the fear is only an illusion. Often when it is faced one says, 'Why was I so afraid?' Like at school, as one faces the issues inside of oneself, one then begins to raise the vibration and move closer to the Source, which many know as God. Face your issues, which are being mirrored for you by those around you. Stop running away and move forward in vibration. Our energy, the energy of the Masters, is always with you to assist you in this endeavour."

LOVE

"What is love? Many have tried to give an answer to this question, and many think they know the answer. Love is the need within you to share with another person, no matter what sex, a closeness, and to give, and receive affection.

The sexual union with two who have no love is just an action. It can please, but it cannot satisfy the soul. Only when one has an open heart and can feel emotion for the person sharing the experience, can the sexual act then become a momentous occasion. When love is in action, it is demonstrated by both partners in the sharing of

77

affection, kindness and consideration to each other. If a partner is ill, then caring for that person becomes a caring experience; if there is no love, it can become a chore.

Everyone on the Earth plane has a need for physical affection; it is a part of your being. If it is denied then the heart closes and the body becomes cold and immobile. When it is touched in affection then it opens like a rose after a cold winter. When one loves another, one does not criticize the other. You accept each other for the uniqueness that you are, two different beings who vibrate to a different tune. Even twins vibrate to their own tune.

All human beings are different to each other. Yet you try to *make* your partner like you! You cling in your relationships and you may manipulate your partner to change. However, when there is love, then you accept your partner for their difference and do not criticize or try to change and manipulate.

If you want to know love, then let go of your fear. Understand that your partner *is* different to you. They cannot be you, and you cannot be them. Accept their uniqueness, and if you cannot, then the partner is not for you. If this is so, move on so that you may experience happiness, and try to maintain friendship in the relationship that has ended. Love comes from the heart centre; it is totally embracing, and for those who feel it, either from another human being or from the Divine Source, they truly know happiness. They also know love."

MARRIAGE

" I have been asked to comment on the subject of marriage within the Spiritual context. First of all, may I say that we in Spirit do not insist on marriage. It is a choice made by humanity. Man made marriage, and it was created mainly for man to have a hold over women. It does not matter whether a child is born in or out of wedlock, it is still loved by God. Its status does not change that.

Over the Earth years, marriage has become a business. It seems the more you can spend on your wedding, the more esteem you have. Yet marriage is not about clothes or cakes or receptions, it is about the commitment of two people to each other.

There are times when, because of karma, two people need to marry, as in the case of my channel Margaret and her ex-husband Peter. They had unfinished business from a past life, where Peter ran away on his wedding night with another woman. In this incarnation he chose to come back and stay, much to his shock when he became aware of this! It created quite a battle within him, and there often is this battle, when there is karma in a relationship. One or the other partner, still wants to run away!

When two people come together, it should be their choice whether they marry or not. We do not insist on this for you. It is your choice. For many years, the church forced it, and any child born out of marriage was labelled a bastard and was made to feel different. God does not see any child as different; they are all His children. If you

79

choose to marry, ask of yourself, do I need all of the ceremony? Often, you will find that you will not. If you do choose the ceremony, make it a Spiritual one.

Often, two people come together to finish karma and later on in life, there is no longer any spark left in the relationship. It is also in order to leave a relationship if you are unhappy. If the karma is not finished in the lessons to be learned, the Universe will bring another partner to learn from again. We have no insistence on anything, you, humanity, choose what you need and what you do. Your astrological chart will indicate if you are to have more than one partner, or if the possibility is there should you not complete the karma with one partner. It is *your* choice."

MILLENNIUM CHANGES

" I n another teaching I have written about the changes to the physical body which are occurring because of the Photon Belt energy.*

Now that the Photon Belt is actually at work in the Universe, enormous numbers of people are experiencing these symptoms. It is due to the cellular changes that are taking place in the physical body at this time. Many souls are making mention of the fact that they are forgetting things. It is not senility, nor what is known as Alzheimer's disease, but it is the cellular part of the body freeing itself from old concepts and ideas. Humanity is destined in the future to live in the *Now*, the *Now* is *this* moment, not the

* see teaching on The Photon Belt

past or the future as you know it on the Earth plane, but just *Now*.

If one thinks in the *Now*, then one is truly in the moment. As the Earth plane changes, as time passes as you know it, much will change on a cellular level. For those of you, and there are many young ones amongst you, I say, do not fear the fact that you have memory loss. It is just your body changing and making way for the new. That is the purpose of the energy of the Earth plane.

There are many other changes taking place also, but have no fear. There will be many who will not experience the changes for they have chosen not to stay on this Earth plane. It is their choice, but for those who stay, change is inevitable. The change must occur for humanity to move forward.

Loss of memory is just one symptom, starting a sentence and then finding one has forgotten what one is talking about is another. It is just cellular change. This is not a permanent situation but it must happen for you to move forward in vibration. More and more souls are awakening to their higher consciousness than ever before. It is designed to move humanity forward and to clear away the old thinking. Just let it happen if it comes to you. It is not permanent and once it is over, you will find yourself in a different energy."

MIRRORS

 "ou are all mirrors for each other. What you see in another that you do not like, or which annoys you, is what *you* need to look at within yourself.

It is an aspect of yourself which is being brought to your attention. It is saying, 'Look, this is what you need to see.' Yet often, you are so frightened you either banish the person from your presence, or you run away from it.

Many of you who are healers, teachers, readers or therapists, often channel so much Spiritual energy that this increases the size of the mirror! You wonder why you do not like a person, when in fact it is yourself that you do not like. Their large stomach, on a subconscious level, reminds you of your own. Their loud laugh is yours. Their embarrassing ways mirror yours. You are looking at yourself and do not realize it.

Often you will laugh at another, or make a joke of something about them. You do not realize that you are doing this to yourself. Think about those you do not like, what is it about them you do not like? It is *this* that you need to look at within yourself.

Until you can understand that *you* are a mirror, and that in another person you see a mirror of *yourself*, you will continue to stumble through life, with no direction, unaware of what it is that you have to look at. Yet, it is right in front of you but you cannot see. You do not see because you don't want to. Yet the person who is the mirror is saying, 'Look at me, I am trying to tell you something, can't you see?' But you are in fear or denial, and cannot do this.

The next time you do not like something about someone, ask yourself, 'What is it that I do not want to see in myself?' You will then be closer to ascension, and to being free of the Earth plane forever."

MONEY

"**Y**ou hold such store on the Earth plane with what you call 'money.' It has become your God! You fear it, envy it, desire it, and yet you do not realize, it is there for all if only you knew the rules to obtain it.

There are many who are on a Spiritual path and they say, 'But to ask for Money is not Spiritual.' Why is it not Spiritual? Should everyone in the world go around like a Buddhist monk with his begging bowl? The Creator gave all of you an abundant supply of energy. However, you are not using the energy in the right way and this is why many of you have problems.

First of all, many of you limit your thinking. You say over and over, 'I will never have enough money,' or other such negative statements. By saying those words and affirming them, *you are creating them!* Many of you carry around the programming of your parents which has been negative. Your parents lack, fear or concern over money can often become yours.

I have said many times, 'A labourer is worthy of his hire.' All humanity is worthy of hire, but many do not know what their worth is. Five Earth years ago I informed my channel to place a worth on herself. She was working for very little money. She was not happy doing this and felt she was not being paid what she was worth. She had studied for years on the metaphysical subjects and paid out much money for books which we had led her to. These became her teaching tools. She could not see the value of her work.

She chose to experience criticism and negativity in her early life to help control the ego that, for many incarnations, had been a problem to her. So she chose her Earth father who did not make life easy for her. He continually told her she was not worthy, that she was 'stupid,' a 'thickhead,' and a 'blockhead.' She did not have a very good opinion of herself. With the help of the Masters, plus that of her husband, we were able to finally release her from the feelings of inadequacy and she finally put a worth on herself.

The Creator gave all of you talents. Those talents can be put to use to earn a living for yourselves, yet many of you do not know where those talents lie. You do not even see that you are worthy to have them. For some, the image of earning and having a lot of money is abhorrent to them; it speaks of capitalism, greed and avarice. Yet with money one can put food on the table, pay the accounts, purchase much needed objects, pay for travel expenses. It is merely a form of exchange for another's energy, whether that energy is material, mental or Spiritual.

I have said many times to enquirers, if you have a good income then tithe to something you believe in. It could be a scholarship for a student who cannot afford it or sponsorship of a child in a country where poverty is great. It may be to your favourite charity or just given to someone you feel needs it, but given anonymously. In that way, one keeps the Spiritual aspect in the scheme of things.

Do not fear money, for it is the essence of all life. Know that *all* humanity can manifest *all* they need and more. However one needs to ask of the Creator, for the Creator does not know what you need until you ask. You cannot assume He does. When you have asked, you then leave it be. You only have to ask once. However if you are doing this, you *must* have positive thoughts about money. If you continue to say, 'I will never have money,' you will create this reality. If you say, 'I will have abundance in my life each day,' you will create this also.

No soul should have to live on welfare, on limited means, to have to live in the streets unless they choose to do so. There is abundance for all. It is just a question of asking and then having the patience to see it manifest. Try it, you will be amazed at what happens.

Stop thinking poor. So what if your parents were, *you* do not have to be so! You can have much abundance in your life. You create each day, with your thoughts, feelings and words, your future reality. Start creating a positive one instead of a negative one. Create your own abundance from this day forward."

MY ARRIVAL

" I am aware that certain souls are awaiting my imminent arrival on this Earth plane. That some souls are even vying to serve me and be by my side when I make my appearance. How idealistic and impractical! My work is not to be done through the mediums of fanfare and ceremony, but as Jesus said, 'Like a thief in the night.' One does not know a thief is around and neither will you. Humanity would not be able to stand my high frequency energy if I were to appear on the Earth plane.

My purpose on the Earth plane is to slowly but surely,

infiltrate those souls who wish to change, to show them another way. A way without fear and guilt and other emotions. To teach the world through the medium of the Internet, and where possible through personal teaching. My words will be there long after my channel has passed on. That is the purpose of the writing. A written reminder, a witness to Truth which will one day be taken seriously.

As humanity moves up in vibration, slowly they will see the bigger picture and the new wisdoms will spread. That is my purpose here, through my channels, one of whom writes my words on this site, the many who do my healing, and others who channel in different ways. They know who they are and do not seek fanfare or fame. They just do their work quietly and unobtrusively. To those souls their rewards are not on this Earth plane, but beyond. The satisfaction of knowing they made a contribution to change. Seeking no reward or recognition but when recognition comes, in giving Spirit the credit not them-selves. This is true service!

I am already here through my channels and have been for some Earth time, many have just failed to notice."

MY ARRIVAL IN CONNECTION WITH THE RAPTURE

"Much has been said about my appearance on the Earth plane. Many have said that I will appear in physical form. Many have said I will come in a cloud, and others have said that I am already here on the Earth plane, and have been for many years. *None of the above is true.*

I cannot appear on the Earth plane, for my vibration is too high. I can however, channel through one on the Earth plane who has been trained for the purpose of taking my energy. Yes, I am a World Teacher, for I teach on this website and it does travel the world. However, I have said many times, I am a messenger; a messenger for one even higher than me, one known as the Ultimate Being or God.

Many have also said that with my coming, or with my appearance, I will collect all the souls who are 'good' and transport them into Spirit in a form of rapture! A state of bliss! This I cannot do, for *all* souls have to go through their own journey to Heaven, and there, they will *not* face God, but they will have to face themselves, without the Self there, without the Devil which is the Self, the Ego. They will see all that they have done in their incarnation.

There can be no rapture until the vision you see is free of negative energy and action, once you have passed into the Spiritual realms. Yes, rapture is possible, but only if one is willing to work at defeating the negative energy within oneself and destroying the ego.

I have chosen to work through channels. There are many who channel my energy; healers, teachers, intuitives, and they can be recognized by the work they do and the miracles they perform in my name and energy. If there are testimonials to their energy and healing, then they are working with me and channel my energy. Those who come into my energy, *feel* it. Many have a rapturous experience while on the Earth plane, which enables them

87

to see and experience the Higher Self, which is in each and every one of you. They do not need to be transported to do this.

I am not living in London, nor anywhere else in the world. I reside in the hearts of my channels. It is there that I do my work."

NATURE

"ou are a part of nature, as nature is a part of you. You were born to be together, to help each other. Nature was created to be the balance for you in this incarnation. To help clean the air through the presence of trees. To provide water to drink and cleanse oneself, as well as to play in. To work in total harmony with all of humanity. In the beginning this was so. All was as one.

Then humanity, in its desire for modernization, found chemicals to alter the food that you eat. Often these chemicals were released into the water, the rivers and streams. It was often done in a way that humanity did not know about.

If only you could see that there is enough for everyone. That God, or the Ultimate Being, provided everything you need, the food, water, herbs, fish and meat. Yet humanity has become obsessed with changing everything you have. It does this to 'enhance' it, to genetically modify the very DNA of God's work.

You are losing your association with nature. If you do not change soon, and return to the way you were, there will be no resemblance at all to the food and water of old. The way it was designed by God.

I am not preaching with my message, just informing; asking you to stay in touch with nature, to cherish it and nurture it. For when you destroy nature, you destroy yourself. You are one with nature and cannot be separate from it."

NOW

"*I* am often asked about certain things in what you on Earth call, 'the past'. About matters to do with things that have long ago become history, as you know it. I often refrain from answering these questions because they deal with something that has been and gone. It is the purpose of the Masters to teach humankind to live in the *Now* and not to think about the past or the future, as you on the Earth plane know it. The *Now* is all that there is.

If you do not live in the *Now*, then you are not living in the moment. One of my channel's clients said that she had difficulty understanding the *Now*. Margaret explained that she lived in the *Now*, did not dwell on the past, because that had been and gone, and she planned for the future. This client said that if Margaret planned for the future, then surely, she was not living in the *Now*? It was a very good question, and one that needs explanation.

Margaret does live in the *Now*, we have trained her to do so. However, she does not allow opportunities that come her way to slip away from her. One of these opportunities came recently, when she was offered a reduction on an airfare for travel later in the year. She could have said, 'no thank you, I am living in the *Now* and will deal with my airfare when the time comes,' but she did not. She looked upon the discount on her airfare as a blessing from the Spiritual realms, and took it.

By living in the *Now* you allow blessings to come to you. You follow your intuition and follow direction that is given to you by your Guardian Soul who is in charge of your life in this incarnation. Margaret does live in the *Now*, but she also listens to the voice within which she knows, after 20 years of listening to it, that it is never wrong and only wants to help her.

One day, this voice told her that in six months time she would be travelling, once again, to the USA and England. Knowing this, she then started preparing for that travel. Because it was meant to be, everything fell into place, even the discount on her travel. She did not worry about anything, just accepted that it would all fall into place, and it did so.

Living in the *Now* is the only place to be, because one is 'living in the moment.' Even the words I wrote a few sentences ago are now passed. By living in the *Now*, one is only aware of this moment, nothing else matters. It takes much training to change old conditioning of living in the past, present, and looking to the future or worrying about it. But once you start to change your thinking and accept the *Now*, then nothing can go wrong, because you allow your destiny to come to you. There is no difficulty! You are just in the *Now*, in the moment, and without fear, worry, doubt, envy, greed, or any negative emotion. You just experience the *Now* in all of its glory. It is the ultimate experience to do so."

OPINIONS

"Are you aware that on the Earth plane, simply by giving your opinion, you can stop another from their destiny or from the enjoyment of something? For instance, it is common practice on Earth that when one has a friend who intends doing something; one tends to say, 'Oh! I did that, and it didn't turn out,' or, 'I wouldn't do that if I were you. I did and it wasn't good.'

How do you know that the person will not enjoy it, or that it will not work out for them? Your opinion may differ from theirs, yet you insist on giving your opinion! Often a person will act on that and miss opportunities. Just by making a comment or giving an opinion you can create karma for yourself. If your opinion or comment stops another from doing something that could enable them to grow, learn lessons or change their path, then you become a negative force in their life, which then creates karma.

It is the same also, if you make comment about someone to another. Often a friend will say, 'I intend meeting John Doe today,' and you, who have perhaps not had a good experience with John say, 'Oh I wouldn't! He is this way inclined or not any good.' By saying this you can perhaps, stop someone from connecting with an important part of their life, or from learning lessons that have to be learned. If one feels anything about anyone or anything, it is best to remain silent rather than make comment or give an opinion.

By being silent one does not create karma. It is the only way to be if one is looking for enlightenment and growth Spiritually. While you make comment and give an opinion, then one stops oneself and others from growing."

PAIN

"You cry aloud in your pain and suffering and you say, 'God, why do you do this to me? I am a good person. I try to help everyone and be kind.' However, you are not aware of what you have done to another in another incarnation, and if this is so, this could now be time for repayment.

All that you sow, you eventually reap. There was once a man who did the most awful things to people in his life. He made money, but did not tithe nor did he share it. He evicted people from his property because he simply did not like them. He treated his wife like a slave, and other family members were put to work like bullocks pulling a plough. He had no remorse and did not seem to suffer in that life. He made a lot of money and died very wealthy. Even when he died, he made provision that his family would not get his money.

In his next incarnation he found himself very poor, being evicted time and again from premises he rented. He and his family were treated worse than animals where they worked, and he could not understand why. He finally called upon God and asked, 'Why am I and my family suffering this way? I try to be a good person, but I cannot take anymore of this pain and suffering.' The Divine Soul then showed him, in a dream, where the pain and suffering came from and he was ashamed. He saw all his past life deeds and was sorrowed to see that what he was receiving in this life, he had given out in another.

This is not the only reason for pain and suffering though. Many souls choose to suffer pain, loss, sadness, illness, and other painful things to enable them to grow or to learn from these experiences to help others. A soul can be a better drug counsellor because he has been a drug addict himself and has suffered the pain of this. All that you suffer and have pain with, is because you choose to go through this. You are either repaying karma, or are learning lessons to help yourself and others. When you feel that you are suffering and in pain, ask yourself why this is happening and allow yourself to be still so that the answer may come. Know that *you* choose it, nobody makes you experience it. It is of *your* own choice.

All pain and suffering is cause and effect. If you look to the positive in your pain and suffering, then it will not seem such a burden to bare. Once you start to look to the positive you will find the problem will disappear or become less than it is.

We, the Lords of Karma, the Ascended Masters, help each one of you choose your incarnations. We, with the Creator, the Divine Soul, help you to choose the lessons for that life by showing you the records of your deeds that have still to be addressed. Sometimes we say to you, 'You will find that situation too much. You may find you cannot go through with it.' But you ignore us and then find yourselves in terrible pain and suffering, crying out for help because you *are* finding it too much to cope with.

God, the Creator, the Divine Soul, is not responsible for your pain and suffering, you are. When you realize this, then it does not become such a burden and it passes quickly. There are no accidents. All that you do is a choice. Only when you have repaid your debts and learned your lessons, do you have no more pain and suffering. This can be done in one incarnation, or it can

93

take many incarnations. You can start now by observing your actions and living a life where you create no negative situation, but only work for the higher good in all that you do. It is *your* choice."

PAST

"So many of you live in the past, in fear of moving forwards, in fear of change.

The past, as you know it, has gone! It has left only memories, some good, some bad, but memories only. You cannot return to the past, you cannot live in the past. How can you live in something that has gone? What you are actually doing is living in memories. Many souls live in their memories because that is where they were happiest. They do not realize that they can have happiness today, in the *Now!* All they can see is their memories. When they do this, they cannot see the *Now* or what is to come, or what you on the Earth plane call the 'future'.

It is hard to break free of memories, but once you are free, then you can live a life that is free, unencumbered, because there is only a *Now*. This moment of time, *Now*, is all that matters, nothing else is important, the *Now* is all. What matters is this moment of time, the *Now*, and allowing what is to come to manifest. If you live in the *Now*, you leave the past behind and allow the future to manifest, then you truly are in line with your destiny. The past has been and gone. It taught you lessons, helped mould you into what you are now, been a blessing or some souls may think it a curse, but it has gone. Do not step backwards into the past, but just be still in the *Now*. When you can do this you will truly know peace.

As you do this, the future as you call it, or what is to come for you, will unfold gracefully, bringing with it wonderful opportunities for growth and expansion."

PAST LIFE INCARNATIONS

" number of souls have written and asked me to explain the phenomena of past lives. Not everyone believes in this phenomenon of course, but for those who do, first of all, I must stress to you that you can have many incarnations. You are a soul on a journey trying to perfect yourself. You incarnate to choose experiences which enable you to grow and enable you to perfect yourself. However, sometimes things do not go the way *you* planned them to. When this happens, and especially if someone else is hurt by these actions, remember, for every action there is a reaction.

When you return to spirit, you make the choice whether you wish to repay the karma on the Earth plane, or whether you wish to work in Spirit to repay this energy. *You* make the choice. If you return to the Earth plane, you choose the experiences and the life you wish to experience. You and *only* you choose this. It can be as easy, or as difficult as you like. *You* choose this. How does she know?

Each incarnation is a separate experience. You can only be one soul in each incarnation. For instance, my channel Margaret cannot return again as Margaret. Being Margaret is unique to her in one incarnation only. She can however, choose to learn lessons *not* learned in this

95

incarnation in another, as another soul. For instance, in a past life, Margaret was a channel like now. She was also a Medium and Healer. She came to assist humanity in its growth. However, she had much fear of ridicule in her work, especially public ridicule. She had much fear also, and although she came to make the teaching simple, she made it very complicated indeed, so much so that once she had written a book, another book was written to explain the first book! She also avoided public work which she had also chosen to do.

Margaret chose to come back to right what she did wrong. And so, in this incarnation, she faced her fears; had to deal with public humiliation in her work, and experienced this in a very public way. She also created the website, and as you can see, the writings she now channels are very simple indeed.

She *cannot* live this incarnation again, because she has learned many of the lessons. Even with souls who do not learn many lessons or face their fears, the incarnation can never be the same again. Each incarnation is unique. After each incarnation the soul chooses whether to return to the Earth plane, or to another dimension, or whether to stay in Spirit and serve in Spirit, to repay debts incurred in the previous incarnation.

A soul can return to any time period. There is no specific order, such as one thinks on the Earth plane. One can, if one wishes, return in an Elizabethan incarnation, or an Egyptian. *You* are the creator of your incarnation.

96 The Higher Self has the memory of past lives, *not* the Self. Until the Higher Self is allowed access above the Self, past life recall is usually impossible to release. This can be

released however, and the energy of this released, by the guidance of a Healer or a person trained in past life therapy. When sufficient Higher Self energy is present, then, and only then, can past life memory be released."

PAST LIVES

"**y**ou have all been here before and some of you will come back again. Inside of you is all the knowledge of the incarnations you have experienced. The more you release the negative energy inside of you, the closer you will come to experiencing those lives.

The World of the Spiritual is your true home where you go to rest in between incarnations. This dimension is a resting place for your soul, before you decide to take further lessons on the Earth plane. The purpose of incarnation is for you to learn lessons, to grow in the Spiritual aspects of yourself.

I am often asked, 'Master can I find out where I am failing to learn?' and I tell souls, yes! It can be found in astrology, in true Spiritual esoteric astrology. You will find all of the answers that you need to help yourself and to help you on your Spiritual path. Find out who you are and what you are here to do again, and you will move forward dramatically.

Eighty percent of your life on this Earth plane is spent in past life memory, yet you are not aware of this. A true Spiritual teacher will be able to tell you where you are spending that eighty percent and which incarnations you are living over and over, as if on a mouse's wheel. Soul

97

growth will occur when you can find out your true self.

Looking at your past life incarnations can enable you to let them go and to move forwards, never to look back again."

PATIENCE

"Humanity today lives in a world where everything is so quick. There is no time to stop and enjoy the smell of a flower, or to see a stream meandering downwards. Life is continual rush and hustle. I am often asked, 'Master, what can I do to become more Spiritual?' and my answer to that is, to have patience. When one is in Spiritual development one is working with us. When we are working with you we cannot rush the work we do. If we did, your human body would not be able to handle the energies that are being generated by us.

There is much we have to do in helping your body change from one vibration to another, this *has* to take time. Yet you on the Earth plane, you are so impatient. You rarely sit down to think, let alone taking the time to become at one with us. We cannot work with you when you are rushing about all the time and do not have the time for us. 'How much time is needed?' I can hear you say. All we need at the most is a regular thirty Earth minutes per day. We do not need you to go into meditation or do anything spectacular, we just need you to sit quietly and to tune into us. This can be done by visualization, or by thinking of us in some way. We just need you to switch off and allow us access to your body. We can then do what is necessary to help you to raise your vibration. It may take a number of Earth years for this to be accomplished.

When students do the Master's course we have a wonderful time, because you are not only with us in our realms, but we also have a chance to work on you a lot quicker than would normally happen. Either way, patience is required while our work is being done. You asked for assistance before you were born from we, in the Spiritual realms, and we offer that assistance. But unfortunately, when you come to the Earth plane, you have forgotten that plea for assistance. It makes our work quite difficult when we cannot work with you. It is said on the Earth plane I believe that, 'patience is a virtue.' It is in a way, because with patience you can raise your vibration and move into a higher energy. Humanity is in fear of sitting still, because when one does start to sit still, usually one has to look at issues that need to be addressed. Fear is the main reason why you cannot sit quiet and still.

However, Spiritual development cannot take place until you are willing to look at yourself in an intimate and personal way. Only then can we show you the imperfections and help you to move out of them. We do so want to help you, but first of all, you have to help yourself."

PEACE

"Since the beginning of time, since man and woman first stepped foot on the Earth, humankind has tried to create a lifestyle, by doing things the way that *they* wanted. This has resulted in ego, selfishness and a lust for control and power. Many prophets have visited the Earth plane with their words of encouragement, change and Spirituality, but their words

99

have been ignored, changed or misinterpreted. The Christian faith was originally a single belief system. Christ taught some wonderful things. By associating with Mary Magdalene and turning the tables of the money changers in the temples, he showed that he was one with the people and not above them. From one simple faith or belief system has now come many thousands of sects, all of them breakaway sections of that first teaching by the Christ.

Each one of them believes that they have the answer. Many knock on people's doors and persuade them to believe in their faith, often using fear tactics to do so, such as the ending of the world. This often results in people turning away even more, from religions and faiths because it interferes with free will. The original teaching of Christ is not in The New Testament that humankind reveres so much. Only a portion is revealed in that book as quite a lot has been misinterpreted through translation or simply omitted by priests. They did not feel that certain words should be included because it would have resulted in people turning away from the church.

The original teaching of Christ, and all of the prophets who have come to the Earth plane since humankind was created, was that *love* is the key; love for the self, love for your fellow man, letting go of fear, doubt and all negative emotions. Become *your* own master by letting go and allowing love into the heart.

With the fishes and the loaves Christ taught about sharing. With Mary Magdalene he taught that you are all worthy of the Divine Soul's love, no matter who you are. With the money changers in the Temple, he taught about greed. In all of the stories of Christ he taught by example, and he enabled humankind, at that time, to learn new ways. All of the other prophets did this too.

He taught equality for all and yet two thousand years later there still exists, on your Earth plane, inequality, greed, fear, and still people have not found the Spiritual within themselves. The words of Christ that were so Spiritual have been changed beyond comprehension. Many look towards the church, but cannot find the answers to their own Spiritual search.

The time has come for humankind to listen to the Spiritual within them. To take back the power they have given to priests and the religious. To understand what life is really all about. To understand that karma plays a major part in life and that *love* is the most important thing. As St Paul said in Corinthians 1-13, 'If you do not have love, you have nothing.'

To make the world a better place, humankind has to turn to the Spiritual within. To learn to free themselves of the Lower Self and allow the Higher Self in. To learn about the Spiritual laws through karma, astrology and the ancient arts which are making a return in this century. This will enable humankind to become master of their own destiny. They will no longer hand power over to others, but have their *own* power to create their own destiny. Sadly, many in the 'new age' movement, as you call it on this Earth plane, do not use the Spiritual part of themselves. Many who do, still need to do a lot of work on themselves to free themselves of the Lower Self and the Ego. Many others though are doing the most wonderful Spiritual work.

Until humankind is in touch with the Spiritual realms within, with the Higher Self, there will never be peace on

101

Earth. Humankind is body, mind and soul; there can be no separation. Find the Spiritual and you will find peace."

PEACE (II)

"Do you have peace in your life? Have you created the perfect life for yourself?

If your answer to this is *No*, then I want you to know that you can have this. Humanity seems to think it has to suffer, that hardship and difficulty are a part of life, but they are not. Each soul has talent; each soul can create a Heaven on Earth that they desire. I can hear you all saying, 'Master tell us how to do this,' and I will.

Let go of your concern for others, give nothing any energy, fear nothing, ask yourself, 'What do I need in life to be happy?' and then create it. It will not happen overnight in Earth time, but it will gradually come to pass.

Humanity has so much fear, fear of losing the job one has, fear of leaving a relationship, fear of debt or hardship. You do not realize that whatever you fear, you draw it more into your energy. Once you let go and say to yourself, 'When I do this, I know Spirit will provide for me,' then it will happen.

Two Earth years ago, I was privileged to teach a woman in New Zealand. She was in a marriage that was not happy and I spoke to her about leaving this relationship, for it was making her life very miserable. As soon as I started speaking to her, I could see her fear! She made all sorts of excuses to stay in the relationship, and I spoke to her no more. She had made her decision. She was in fear of having nothing, of being destitute. The fear was worse than her desire. The fear won.

Eventually this woman became a Spiritual reader and started to realize that she *could* leave and that the longer she stayed, the longer her health was a problem.

Later on she left her husband and surprisingly, all she feared did not happen. Now she has a lovely small apartment, is earning money, and has everything in her apartment she could want. It has all fallen into place because she realized that Spirit would take care of her. She started walking through her fear. She is now experiencing peace in her life. Yes, she still has fear but it becomes less each day.

You too can create peace in your life. Look at your life, where do you not have peace? Start working with that negative energy and you will find that when you change it, you will change too. You will also find peace."

POSSESSIONS

"hy do you hold on to what you have? All that you have is given by the Creator on loan for this incarnation. You can never own it, only use it for this lifetime. Once you pass into the Spiritual realms, and leave your mortal form behind, so will you leave all that you own.

You can say, 'but I have worked for what I own,' and I will say to you, 'Yes, this is true, but you have just exchanged energy for energy, nothing is *ever* yours forever.' Take only in this incarnation what you need. Do not allow your life to be tied down with belongings and possessions. The less that you have, the more energy that can flow around you. The more you tie yourselves down with possessions, the more you tie yourself to the Earth plane and stop the flow of energy around you.

Look around you, at your possessions. What do you have that you no longer need? What are you accumulating that another could use? You hang onto things, like a dog with a bone, hoping that one day you can use it. The less that you have, the more you can attract to you. If you have possessions that you do not use, and hold on to them because one day you may need them, knowing *also* that day will never come, then the more you hold yourself from abundance. All that you have is energy in material form. As you let go of all that you do not need, the more you open the door for more. When you hold onto your possessions because of fear, or lack in the future, then the energy around you becomes stagnant, still, and cannot move. Therefore you hold back the flow of energy.

Let the energy in your life flow. Do not hold onto anything, or anyone. Once you do this, then you will experience an abundance that you have never experienced, and you will find all that you need flows to you without effort."

PROPHETS

"Over thousands of Earth years, the Creator has sent to the Earth plane, messengers to carry His word. To bring to the Earth plane much change in the way humankind conduct their affairs. Your holy books are filled with stories of humans, male and female, who became the mouthpieces for this energy. Jesus Christ was one of them, Mohammed another. In fact all of the prophets who have been written about, including many females such as Joan of Arc and Saint Bernadette of Soubirous, have all carried the word of the Creator, or have been associated with holy figures that have appeared to them and given them the message of the Creator.

The messengers have talked about leaving the negative behind, such as fear, greed, ego, pride and many other emotions that stop humankind from reaching the higher part of him, his Higher Self. They talk of love as being the only key to happiness, and of replacing hatred and anger with love. The man Jesus was such a man. He chose to be born to carry the word of the Spiritual realms, with the help of the Creator. He was not the 'Son of God,' but a 'Messenger of God.' He was able, with the Holy Spiritual Energy, the Creator's energy, to heal the sick, counsel the weak and troubled, and transfigure those in the world of the Spiritual, through him. His disciples saw him transfigure, and because of his Spiritual energy, he was able to show people the power of God, the Christos or the Christ Soul. He was born Jesus. It was only later, that he was called Jesus the Christ, and then just Christ.

Many souls on this Earth plane today have those same gifts

105

that Jesus had; they too can heal, transfigure, and counsel through Spiritual energy those who are troubled and weak. He was simply a man who carried the word of God, the Creator, as were all the other prophets who came before and after him.

Their purpose was to change the thinking of humankind and help them to uplift their thoughts and raise their vibration to connect with their Higher Self. All of the messengers had followers who became their disciples. All of them had disciples who betrayed them or turned away from them, even young Bernadette Soubirous was ridiculed and laughed at. So too was Joan of Arc because she had visions and heard voices. Jesus was crucified and all the other prophets have met their end in saddened circumstances.

How do you know what Jesus looked like and what he said? The book you call The Bible, the New Testament, has been translated many times and during those many times, words have been changed. Yes, there was written proof; St Paul wrote to the Corinthians, but he wrote in the language of the time, not English, so many of his words, thousands of years ago, were changed or omitted due to translation problems. Many of the Disciples of Jesus, Matthew, Mark, Luke and John, passed on their experiences by word of mouth. A lot of what they spoke about was also changed, and it was the same with all the other prophets.

Jesus was a member of a group called the Essenes, a secret order who were experienced in the act of white magic or

ritual. The Essenes knew of many things to do with the Spiritual and how to use the Spiritual realms to help them in their lives. Jesus was versed in Astrology through the

Essenes, and was quite aware of reincarnation and the return of the soul to learn lessons. When he told Lazarus to pick up his bed and walk, he knew that there was nothing wrong with Lazarus. Lazarus was faking illness. When Lazarus realized that Jesus knew he was not sick, he then picked up his bed and walked, and that of course, to everyone gathered around Jesus, seemed a miracle.

Much of what has been written in your Holy Book about Jesus is not what happened; it has been changed many times over the years. How do I know this? Because in the Spiritual realms, we have the gift of all knowledge. It is time that humankind realized that what has been written in the past is not true, and that it has been changed over the years. Sometimes, not only for humankind to gain control over his fellow human, but also to help keep the role of female humans in a subservient position. There have always been those who had visions, who saw things clairvoyantly. Many are born with this gift, yet over the years they have been persecuted for the use of these gifts and called witches and evil ones. Yet St Paul, in his letters to the Corinthians, talks of the gifts of the Spiritual and exhorts humankind to, 'seek ye the Spiritual gifts, especially that you may prophesy.'

It is these humans who we, in the Spiritual world can use to convey the message of the Creator. They have the ability to communicate with a Higher Source, just as Jesus did, and to channel the messages we send to help humankind on their path to a higher vibration. Jesus and the other prophets brought the teaching of how to raise your vibration, and of how to cancel out future incarnations on the Earth plane. They brought the keys to help humankind understand the Spiritual part of

107

themselves, and enable them to become the master of their own destiny. Those in power did not like this and set about destroying, not only the prophets, but often ridiculing them as well. These brave souls suffered much for the work they did, but their words today and their message is still known. In some cases, many thousands of years later, they are revered for their courage and loved for their sacrifice.

There are many now that are prophets. They speak of Spiritual realms and they too can heal and display incredible Spiritual powers. We do not send one human, we send many, and they are all around your Earth plane at this period of Earth time. They are light workers of a very high vibration. It is the intention of these souls to help those who want to become the master of their own destiny; to give them the knowledge to take back their own power, and not give their power to another soul. Those who take back their own power will become beacons of light and eventually, the Earth plane will be filled with these souls shining so brightly that even the dark side of life cannot stand to be among them, because their love and their light will overcome the darkness.

This will not happen overnight, but it will happen slowly, and eventually. There will be a new Earth, a new age of peace, love and contentment. Many souls will have to go through very difficult times for this to happen, but it will happen, and then there will truly be a new Heaven and a new Earth, and each human will become a Master in control of its own destiny."

PUT GOD FIRST

"You say to me, 'How can I get rid of the Self?'
My answer to you is, 'Put God first.'

You say to me, 'How can I become more Spiritual?'
My answer to you is, 'Put God first.'

You ask of me, 'How can I raise my vibration?'
My answer to you is, 'Put God first in your life.'

When God, the Divine Intelligence, or whatever you call that energy, is in your life, then the Self has no control. You see, the Self is in fear of God and of the energy of God. It is the only force in the Universe that the Self will not fight. The reason why? Because God has no fear and the Self lives and feeds on fear. When God is there, first in your life, there is no room for Self."

QUESTIONING

"Why do you question so much? I will tell you why, it is the Self who questions. The Higher Self has all the answers and will provide them when they are needed. The Self needs to know how, why, what, when. When you question you stop the flow of inspiration from the Higher Self. If only you would sit back and relax, allow the mind to be still, the answers will come. Each one of you has the answers to all of life inside of you. Each one of you has an attachment to the Ultimate Being. However, because of the mind, because of logic, you cannot get the answers from the Source.

The Self is the connection to self-preservation. It loves the comfort zone. It does not want to change and so, it creates question after question in order to stop you moving forward. It will also make excuse after excuse for you not to move forward, and many of you listen and follow like sheep. When you do not question, but trust that the Universe will lead you to where you have to go and inform you what you have to do, then that is true Faith. The Self however, will say, 'Why are you not doing this? When are you going to do that? You cannot afford to do that, etc, etc.' Yet, the Higher Self will say 'Let me bring it to you, sit back, relax, don't worry, it will happen.' When this happens, and you allow it to happen, you are truly in Spirit."

RELIGION

"It saddens us, we the Masters, to see what has happened in the name of religion on the Earth plane today. The word of God was brought to the Earth plane to help humankind and yet it has become the purpose of war and dissension.

Why can you not understand that each of you is an individual with your own belief system? You were created different to each other. No two people are the same, even twins are different. Because of this fact, you cannot all have the same belief system. If you did you would be like sheep or cattle; instead you are a unique individual. When you can understand that you are different to the person next to you, and that it is alright to be different to that person, only then will you find peace.

You cannot force your ideas on another, either by war or

by force. It is normal to be different; each one of you can have a different belief system to the other and yet still live in harmony and peace. There is only one God, and yet that energy does not care how you worship it, it just asks you to understand the Spiritual part of you, and to work with that part of you to enable you to have a better life.

What does dissension in a belief system do anyway? All it does is kill, maim, injure and create hatred. That is not what God is about. The Divine Being is about love, pure love, and unconditional love for all humanity, man and woman, Hindu and Buddhist, Christian and Muslim, each with their own belief system, yet working side by side for a better world.

When you learn to tolerate each other and respect another's belief system without conditions, then you are on your way to making a better world and creating peace on Earth."

RESPECT

"Until each soul can learn respect for each other, whether it be for their belief, or their partner or colour of their skin, humanity will not have peace in the world. Respect is one of the foremost necessities for peace on the Earth plane. What does it matter that your neighbour is a Jew, Gentile, or New Age soul? That is what they choose to believe. Just because you choose to believe something different does not mean that you cannot get along with each other. If you cannot get *111* along, you will just have to respect them for their differing opinions.

In Spiritual development, respect is one of the most important things to learn. Humanity has a habit where each soul feels it is their duty to change a person's thinking to their own. This is evident in Christian circles where people go and knock on people's doors to try and convert them.

You could say to me, 'but Master, you are doing that with this website, your views are there for people to see,' and I say to you, *yes*, but the choice is given for people to read and then either believe, or dis-believe. No-one calls you and tries to change your thinking. It is your choice.

Respect is the most important ingredient in your lives today. If you do not agree with another, do not waste energy arguing with that person. What a waste of energy! Just say to yourself, 'well, that is their choice and belief, but it is not mine,' and let it be. Give it no more energy. It will aggravate you for a short while, but eventually, you will find that you will accept that person for who they are, not for what they believe in. Soon, in time, their belief system will be unimportant. Learn *respect* and you are on your way to ascension."

SEXUALITY

"There is much discussion in the world today about what is right and wrong with regards to sexuality. There is so much fear and guilt about having a desire for the same sex person. Many consider this an abomination. Why do they do this? They do so, because they do not understand the meaning of love, and are conditioned with thousands of years of belief that humanity should be male and female.

How do you know that what is written is true? Many quote the scriptures from many years ago, but how do you know that this is truth? You do not! Yet because of the power of belief, fear is generated by being different. Many souls returning to the Earth plane and preferring a partner of the same sex have often had that partner in a past life as the opposite sex.

Many years ago, my channel met a woman who was a lovely soul. This woman came to love my channel, but because of her conditioning at that time, my channel ran away. How many of you have run away from a similar situation? Why do you run? You run because you fear, and you fear because you do not understand your feelings and because *society* says it is wrong! It is not wrong. Yes, a woman was designed for childbirth and the male for seeding, but the human body was also designed for pleasure, and how that pleasure is enjoyed is the responsibility of each individual soul. No soul should judge another because of their differences.

When you judge another, you become the judge and jury. Yet how do you know that was not you in a past life or will be in a future life? For those who choose a partner of the same sex, let go of your fear, let go of your loathing of yourself. Honour yourself in your uniqueness. Release the guilt. Enjoy your difference, for you are truly *free*. You have stepped outside the boundaries of conditioning. Once you free yourself, then you can truly be individual. For you truly know love and do not limit it to one sex.

113

If you are one who prefers the opposite sex, then so be it. Enjoy that experience too, but do not condemn another for their choice. How do you know that your choice is right? You do not, only conditioning makes it this way. The only truth is the *Now*, all that has happened in the past is of the past, irrelevant. Let go of the persecution of yourself. Do not waste energy on debating or thinking what is right or wrong. For there is no such thing, only choice."

SILENCE
(Listen to your Soul)

"Why are you afraid of silence? You live in a world filled with noise. There is very little quiet in your lives. In silence, you can listen to the soul. In silence, you can speak to God. This does not mean that you have to sit in silence, stiff and upright. No, it means that you need to be aware of the quiet and not be afraid of it.

When you are quiet you really do have to look at issues around you. If you are on a Spiritual path, it is a time for the soul to show you what needs to be looked at; it may be vanity, anger, frustration and ego to name a few. When you are silent, you can see these in their full glory.

My channel had a friend once who would not be still. She found something to do each and every minute of every Earth day. She wanted to be Spiritual, yet she would not take any time for contemplation or to sit quietly and let the soul speak to her. One day she became very ill, so ill she was forced to go to bed. She could not move for days, and during this time she was in silence most of the time. In the silence her soul spoke to her. This created a healing within her that lasted for many days, more than she anticipated. She experienced anger, pain, hurt, frustration, but for her it was a cleansing; freeing her body of trapped negative energy. She cried the tears of healing.

Each day now she takes thirty Earth minutes to sit in silence and to listen to her soul. She knows that if she does not, she could be forced to do so again, just like before.

Sitting in silence does not mean one has to become like a Buddhist Monk or Nun. For those souls, they make a choice to experience that lifestyle and meditate in that way. For you though, just be in silence. You can read a book or do something in the home, or go for a walk, but it has to be in silence; talking to no-one and listening to what comes into the consciousness from the soul. As Earth time passes, you will find that your soul starts to speak to you, informing you of what is necessary for your growth. If you have no fear and allow the messages to come, you will be the recipient of much healing within yourself.

When one sits still in silence for the first time, the Self becomes impatient and will probably want to move around or try to talk to you. Ignore this. Concentrate on a beautiful scene such as walking in a forest of pine trees, cool and refreshing, on a hot summer afternoon, or a lake with a boat, with you in the boat sailing to an island where there is total peace. Make your own scene where you can be still and silent. Doing this on a daily basis, one can finally listen to the soul."

SO YOU PROFESS TO BE SPIRITUAL

"So, you profess to be Spiritual. Are you the person who will not walk away from an argument because you must prove you are right? Do you make comment on others as to their way of life and their dress? Do you bemoan your lot and blame others for your problems?

If you answered 'yes' to one of those questions, then you cannot profess to be Spiritual. You see, a Spiritual person has no judgment and does not blame others for their problems; has no hate in their heart and does not have to justify themselves to anyone. So many souls think that the path to the Spiritual is easy. They expect reward and material possessions. Being Spiritual means letting go of all material needs, trusting that the Spiritual realms will bring all that you need and having total faith. You can say, 'but Master, if I let go I will have nothing,' and I will say to you, 'when you let go, we can then provide.'

Letting go of the Self is the hardest lesson of all. Accepting the Spiritual world is also very hard too. If you profess to be Spiritual, you will allow us in the Spiritual realms to help you. There is no need for effort, or to even try, because we will lead you and guide you every step of the way. You just have to hold our hand without fear and without doubt. When you can do that, then you can say you are Spiritual."

SOUL GROWTH

"The purpose of your life on the Earth plane is to grow in the Spiritual, to perfect the soul and leave the Earth plane behind. Until you can clear away all the negative programming from the many incarnations you have had, you will continue to come back.

Often you do not know why you are here on the Earth plane. You wonder why life is so difficult, why your dreams are not fulfilled. If you are surrounded in conscious and sub-conscious negative programming, you will continue to have that difficulty.

We come and channel through humans who offer to work with us, to help teach you how to let go; to help you in your soul growth. Those who work with us go through a very hard training to make sure they are worthy to do the work. Often they are abused and hurt by those they try to help. The path of working with us is not an easy one at all. For the few souls who listen, their lives can change and they can move forward in soul growth, often never coming back to the Earth plane again.

At this time of channelling this communication, at the beginning of the new millennium, more souls than ever are searching for their soul growth. Many cannot make it though, because their fear and doubt is stronger than their desire for growth. We can help you, but you need to listen and to implement the changes that are necessary. Often you do not know where the negative programming is inside of you. This is where those trained in the

117

Spiritual, those trained by us, can help you find the answers.

There are quite a few on this website who have completed their studies and who are ready to help you. The final decision lies with you. If you want soul growth, you need to work with us and not have fear. If you can do that, then you will leave the Earth plane behind and move forward.

We are always there to help you, you have to want to help yourself."

SPIRITUAL LAW

"Just as there are laws made on the Earth plane, so there is Spiritual law. It is law which is not man-made, but by God. Laws are teachings which are supposed to help humanity with guidelines to behaviour.

On the Earth plane, law changes constantly with the changes of government or dictator. On the Spiritual level, each generation is given a new law to suit the energy that generation creates. For instance, the law of The Old Testament, as it is known, is not suitable for this day and age, for humanity has changed so much since that time. As humanity progresses and changes, so does the law. The Divine Being, God, is constantly in a state of renewal. It is aware of all that you are doing and of why you are doing it. You can lie to yourself, but not to that Energy. With this in mind, it constantly updates the law so that each generation will have a guide. It is for this reason that there are so many differences in the law over the Earth years. Occasionally, there will be more than one change in a century because humanity changes so much.

I carry the message for the new law. It speaks of becoming one's own Master, of reverence to all faiths, of respect for each soul and their beliefs; that each soul become their own person, responsible for their own actions, decisions and life.

You are the most important person in this incarnation. Yet so many of you become concerned with others, sometimes interfering in their lives and stopping them from growing. While you are involved with others you cannot grow yourself.

The law of this time is different to other laws because the Divine Being, God, can see that until humanity can understand one's Higher Self, one can never be at peace. It is the time for humanity to take responsibility for their own lives and leave others to live theirs. The Spiritual Laws I bring from this beautiful energy are not connected to, *'Thou shalt not'*. That was the teaching of the past, or the interpretation of that teaching. It restricted humanity and stopped its growth. The new law, or teaching, is designed to speak to each man's soul.

For those who are ready and have no fear of change, it will speak to their heart. For those who have fear of change, it will be as if I am the Devil itself. In the future of Earth time, there *will again* be new laws, there *will* be other messengers. As humanity grows, the need will be there for change. One thing is certain and that is the fact that nothing stays the same. Humanity can try and keep it that way, but the Universe will constantly move, which in turn, will bring that change."

SPIRITUAL WRITINGS

"Many people have written to me and asked about writings purported to be 'channelled' from Spirit. Over the many years of Earths occupation by humanity, many souls have been in touch with the Spiritual part of themselves and have communicated with The Ultimate Being. Many of these souls have felt they were being channelled by Spirit or by God, but have written from ego.

The measure of the channelling is the content and the message. Does it speak to your heart? Do you identify with it in your soul? If this is the case, then it is truly channelled. How many people have said the writings or the teachings have helped them? Do not let fear come into your being. Trust from the heart and soul and you will have your answer.

All souls communicate with God, or the Ultimate Being, but only a few can channel and produce the energy to transform, change and enable humanity to help itself. These souls have the destiny to do this. Their energy can move mountains; they are truly of the Divine.

If the message is about the messenger, then look elsewhere. For it is the message, not the messenger that is important."

SPIRITUALITY

"What is the true meaning of Spirituality? It is a word that is much misunderstood. I talk not of the dictionary meaning of the word, but the Spiritual meaning. To be Spiritual, or to have Spirituality in one's life means that one is at peace. You are not only at peace in the physical form, but at peace in all subtle bodies, physical, emotional, mental and Spiritual.

So many of you, when you are confronted with another questioning your actions or the way you do things, feel as if you have to justify yourselves. Either you spend hours putting your point of view across to the person concerned, or write long letters explaining why you are right. Why do you do this? What do you achieve by doing this? Does this change the person's mind? It does not, because the person has already made their mind up about you and have formed an opinion, nothing you say or do will change that. Often times that opinion will be because of a past life experience, where the person concerned sees you as you were, in another incarnation, not as you are now. They judge you because of the past. You cannot change this either, if they choose to do so.

Your Higher Self will know though, and that is all that matters. It is the Self that wants to justify itself, to put its point of view and to defend itself. The Higher Self knows the truth. It is as simple as that, and if you give the situation no energy, then it will disappear whence it came. However, you will have learnt lessons from the experience and that is the primary reason it has come into your space, to teach you lessons. Giving it no energy allows you to

121

move onto other things; to put your energy where it is needed, not with trivial things.

Many have said to me over the years in public channelling, 'Master how can I be more Spiritual?' or, 'Master, how can I raise my vibration?' I have said to them, 'Be at peace with yourself. Concern yourself with nobody else. If another does not like you, that is their problem not yours. Do not give any problems any energy and you will then find peace.'

It is so simple, and yet you find it so hard to do. Many generations ago you were warriors. You had to fight to survive because you knew no other way. Now you do know a better way! Lay down your arms and give it no energy and it will truly disappear. You will then know peace. Do not involve yourself with other's affairs, just with your own, and by doing so you will be free of conflict."

SPIRITUALITY AND SEXUAL ENERGY

" ne of the most important subjects on a soul's Spiritual path is the one on sexual energy. Many souls ask, 'How can I raise my vibration? How can I reach the highest levels of awareness?' Without opening up the Kundalini, and the burning away of the Etheric web at the base of the neck, with the Kundalini fire, higher Spiritual awareness will always be denied.

Many Yogis do manage to raise the Kundalini. It can be raised by meditation over many years of discipline. However, all one needs is the right partner, the right energy, and raising the Kundalini to burn the Etheric web to create a higher state of consciousness.

Even when one has the right partner, raising the Kundalini can be very difficult to attain because most people in the western world are not aware of how important sexuality is to Spiritual growth. Many souls are unaware of the importance of having all of the chakras open and the energy flowing, with regard to their Spiritual growth.

Many male energy souls have no idea of how to please their partner, how to prepare her for the raising of the Kundalini, and many women are just as ignorant.

Once, it was the responsibility of the Priests and Priestesses to educate the male and female souls in the art of pleasure, for that is what the sexual act is. Yet for many souls on the Earth plane today, the sexual act lasts for a few minutes and many souls are left wondering what all the fuss was about. Yet, true Spiritual sex, which is also known as Tantric sex, can be a very beautiful experience. It opens the base chakra, and in turn all the other chakras, to allow the true flow of energy throughout the subtle bodies.

There are many Spiritual souls in the world today who are practicing their arts of healing, counselling and clairvoyance therapies who have actually never opened the Kundalini. They have never experienced the fire raging up the spinal cord to sever the Etheric web, which once broken, keeps the connection of vitalizing Spiritual energy to the throat, brow and crown charkas flowing.

There are very few who can teach of this, and so human-kind stays in darkness, unaware that their Spirituality can be hastened by the raising of the Kundalini.

Over the years, humankind has forgotten the purpose of the sexual energy. They have not learnt of the connection between sexual energy and the chakras, and have been in darkness. It is the most important teaching that one can learn on the path to raising the vibration and the consciousness. For those souls who do achieve this, they become one with the Creator and finally have communion with the Infinite."

SUFFERING

"ou believe that you have to suffer, but you do not. You cry out loud, 'This is my karma!' Yet you do not have to face that karma and suffer. It is how you live it that makes the difference. The soul is on the Earth plane to free itself from many errors of the past. If one looks for the positive message in each situation, then there is no suffering. Let me tell you a story.

My channel Margaret was married to a very nice man. She had a good marriage until she decided to become Spiritual. Her husband did not like her doing this and so made life difficult for her. He would not answer her business telephone and he was rude to her clients or would ignore them all together.

Then one day, after much contemplation, my channel realized that her marriage was not going to work. She could not give up her Spiritual path. Her children had grown and left home, and it was time for her to move ahead with her life. So she then left her marriage.

124

Through intuition, we put the thought in her consciousness to visit a friend of hers who was very intuitive.

Through this friend, we informed her that her husband would do one last thing out of anger, and she was to walk away and not look back when this happened. Months later, her ex-husband went into their business and removed everything of value while my channel was travelling in another town. A few days later, he went to the bank and took all of the money out of their account. My channel heard about this from her manageress who went into the shop to find it empty. Days later she went to the bank for money to pay accounts and there was nothing there.

My channel was devastated. She thought to herself, 'Why did Spirit not help me?' She was angry with us because she thought we had created the suffering. We did not. She had the choice of seeing it as a blessing or as a curse. For many months she was angry with us, yet we had done nothing. We could not have stopped her ex-husband from doing what he did, but we did give warning that it was to happen.

Reluctantly my channel moved forward. Destitute, she had to borrow money to pay her accounts. But we made sure that a friend was there, close at hand to help her with this. All the money she needed was there and her friend assured her that she did not care if it was ever paid back.

When her ex-husband pursued her for the motor car she owned, she decided that he would never leave her alone and so, made the decision to go overseas for a while. It was the saddest day of her life when she made that decision because she did not want to leave. She had nothing. Her new business partner paid for their airfares because she could not pay for them.

She had given her ex-husband all of the household

furniture because she did not need it with her travelling. She had nothing left. This, to her, was indeed suffering. She *did* have faith though, that there was a reason for what had happened.

One year later, my channel had become a radio and magazine clairvoyant in the new country, and was earning far more income than she had done in the shop. She was very successful. All that she had lost was replaced within two Earth years, and from her experience with her ex-husband, she learned so many lessons.

The most important was to walk away and not look back, to keep moving forward, and not go backwards. For the future is always better than the past. If only humanity could see that. But often they cannot. They hold on to all that they have, afraid to let go, not trusting that the Universe will right the wrong. Yet, letting go of the past is the only way to move forward into the light.

Within one year of her moving away, my channel telephoned her ex-husband and thanked him for his actions. She could finally see that, had she stayed the way she was she would still be there, as my channel puts it, 'Still plodding along.' Instead, she had become successful.

You can either see situations that happen to you as positive experiences to learn from, or wallow in self-pity. It is *your* choice. *You choose* whether you suffer or not. The next time something bad happens to you, remember that nothing happens that is not meant to improve your life and assist you to move forward. You just need to have faith that there is, as you say on the Earth plane, 'A bigger, brighter picture."

SURROGACY

"**S**urrogacy is a subject that has many people confused on the Spiritual aspect of it. I have been asked on occasion, how do *we* in the Spiritual Realms feel about this? My answer to that is that there is nothing wrong with it. There are many who, through their karma, have to know the desire to have a child. There are many souls who choose to go through difficulty in having a child.

There are souls who do not wish to have a male partner. I prefer to call these people 'free people', because they are free in their choice. Humanity calls these people homosexuals and lesbians. We give no labels in the Spiritual realms. If a soul chooses to have a partner of the same sex, why should they not have a child? For so long, humanity has been bound by what is right and what is wrong, but, what is right and wrong? Who says what is right and what is wrong? Only the soul concerned knows in their heart this answer. Nobody else has the right to make a decision on it.

There is a saying on your Earth plane, 'There is no greater love, than the love of one who lays down his life for his friend.' I would like to say, 'There is no greater love than one who provides a child for a childless couple.' If it were not meant to be it would not be possible. But it is possible because it is meant to be. It is just humanity in general who, set in their old fashioned ways, cannot see that it does not matter who parents the child. It is *who* looks after the child that is of concern. Two people who love each other, whether of the same or different sex, can make wonderful parents.

Humanity is changing. In a lot of countries in the world single parent families are very much a way of life. Many children have no father or no mother, and sometimes neither. As time passes, this will become more common. Humanity is changing its attitude about surrogacy, and the more that is understood about it in a Spiritual way, the more it will be accepted.

It is love that counts, nothing more. For two souls who want a child, and use a surrogate, either for carrying the child or for providing the sperm for that child, their love for that child is so strong because the child is really wanted.

It is not the conditions, the parents, even the surroundings, it is the love that counts."

TALK

"Do you realize how much *your* talking can cause trouble? Do you realize you have the power to create positive or negative energy on the Earth plane with your words? How often have you said words that were unkind or untrue? 'Isn't her dress awful! Have you seen how she does that! He does that all of the time!' such simple statements but they can have devastating effects. Change the wording though and it is completely different, 'Her dress is unusual but it's not to my taste! That's her way of doing things, but it isn't mine! I don't think he realizes, he does that all of the time!' The energy becomes totally different.

Humanity has become so careless with words. The majority of you never think before you speak. You never consider how your words will affect people. Once they are spoken they cannot be reclaimed. People have even created new karma in their lives because of the words they say.

If the Earth plane is to change and peace is to reign in all areas of life, humanity will need to change this aspect of itself. There is so much talk that is unnecessary, negative and nasty. In relationships especially, words can be destroying and devastating. I understand when you are in pain you find it hard to control your feelings and your words, but unless you do, you will continue to keep making the same mistakes.

So you do not like your friends' clothes or the way they dress. Yet you *have* to make mention of it. Why? Is it because you have always done that? Perhaps your parents did it and they have passed the trend on to you. Perhaps it is for attention. Perhaps you dislike the person and want vengeance. Whatever the cause, it can change!

Think before you speak. Watch *your* words. Is what *you* say of *your* truth? Are you uttering words of comfort, confidence and positive energy? If you find yourself not in this group and want to change, start today. Just be aware of what you are saying each and every moment of the day. Do not expect to change every statement immediately. It will take time to change *all* that you say or utter, but you can start one statement at a time, one word at a time. By doing this, your awareness will allow you to see exactly what you are doing. Do not feel angry, confused or guilty because you cannot change immediately or you keep messing up, as you say on this Earth plane, 'Just keep going forward, one step at a time.' As you do, you will then make the changes necessary in every way."

129

THE
ANTI-CHRIST

"On my travels with my channel Margaret, I have been asked often about the Anti-Christ. Who and what is this energy whom many believe to be on the Earth plane today? The Anti-Christ is a sum total of all that is negative in the world today.

Just as there is light and those who work in the light, there are those who prefer the darkness. Their belief is that they are in truth, but they are in their illusion. They do believe that they are right, and that those in the light, who are positive and happy, are wrong.

Anyone who judges and has hate in their heart, fear in their mind, doubt in their being, are working for that negative energy, the Anti-Christ.

I can see many of you saying that you have fear and doubt, but do not hate, so you cannot be with the negative, but you are, *yes* you are. Your negative fear and doubt assist and aid the energy of the Anti-Christ. The Anti-Christ *is* an energy. An energy made up of the collective thought of anyone who is negative.

Just as there is the Ultimate Being, the God of the Light, there is the God of the dark, the Anti-Christ. The more positive you are the less fear you have, the more faith that you have, the more you support the Light and the more you will move forward in vibration and raise your consciousness.

Imagine an energy cloud in space, moving along, picking up energy from all areas that are negative, getting bigger and bigger like a snow ball. That is what the Anti-Christ is doing. It feeds on people's fear. While people have fear, it has power! The more power it has, the more it wants!

What can be done to over-ride this negative energy? I will tell you, it will not be easy.

First you must remove all fear from your being. Then you must have total faith in all that you do, and no doubt that, what you do *will* happen. This is the only way to fight the negative energy. While you have these negative traits, you cannot be in the light, for the darkness of negativity blinds the light of good and God and shuts you off from the Spiritual realms for a time. The length of this time will depend much on you. But ask for help and we will do all we can to assist you break free from the negativity that you find yourself in. It is your choice!"

THE
CHRIST SOUL

"Many ask, 'How can I become a perfected being?' I say to you, strive for perfection yet know that while on this Earth plane, that perfection is difficult to attain. This is because you are limited by astrological patterning. All of you have planets in your astrological make-up that control your lives. Mercury governs speech and communication, Venus the home and family, Mars ones fighting instinct, etc. It is this that stops one from becoming a perfected human being. While on this Earth plane, you are under control of these planets and they become limiting. It is life after life that perfects the soul and enables the soul to be

131

perfected. Each lifetime is a lesson in becoming perfect until there comes a time that no return to Earth is necessary. Then one becomes perfected.

What is the Christ Soul? It is the essence in man that has total compassion and understanding for their fellow man. It is that part of man that never judges; that has complete understanding of any situation. It is kind and tolerant and yet, it will not stand idle and be walked upon. As Christ himself overturned the tables of the money changers; he did not stand by and do nothing when greed was apparent. That essence is free of ego and completely unbiased. Everyone has the Christ Soul; it is in all people, but it has to be discovered. When man has freed himself of all limitations and conditioning, then he will find the Christ Soul within himself.

Deep within the human psyche is a love that surpasses all barriers. That love can be buried for many centuries. Lifetime after lifetime, as the Lower Self controls the soul, many mistakes are made. The love that is buried can stay buried like a seed that has been planted but is waiting for rain to shoot out and grow to full bloom. Finally though, the Higher Self that has been continually dominated by the Lower Self, starts to fight back and demands to be noticed. When this happens, love, like the small seed, starts to shoot out. If it can be left alone and unhindered by the Lower Self, it will grow so big that it can encompass the world.

Christ said, 'Be as little children.' By this He meant that as a child, life is uncomplicated, unburdened and free. As adults, we burden ourselves with conditioning and habits; some that have been with us most of our lives. When we rid ourselves of these habits and the conditioning, then we can once again become, 'as little children.' Free to see what is around us, and free to hear the words of the Spiritual realms. Free to enjoy our lives as they should be lived, with happiness and without burdens.

When finally, the soul strives for freedom and seeks a higher level of consciousness, there comes a battle between the Lower Self and the Higher Self. The Lower Self has been in charge most of your Earth life. The Higher Self is the part of you that is becoming enlightened. The Lower Self does not want to give up control. It is when this happens that ego purification has to take place. For many months and sometimes for years, the soul is confronted with the Lower Self battling to retain control. The Higher Self becomes stronger and more in control and finally the ego, the 'I' part of us that will *not* give in, finally succumbs to defeat. Only then can the soul find true enlightenment and become one with the Divine Source.

What is the Lower Self? It is pride, selfishness, greed, ego, fear, hatred, and many more negative emotions. What is the Higher Self? It is love, truth, selflessness, honesty, compassion, understanding, non-prejudice, and many more positive emotions.

Which one is in control of you?"

THE EMOTIONAL BODY
(ASTRAL BODY)

 "aster, how can I raise my vibration?" I am often asked. This can be done in many ways; by removing blocks that you have set

in this incarnation and others, and also in working to remove the emotional body. The emotional body is connected to the Self. There is nothing the Self likes more than a good drama. It can have this when it uses and triggers the emotional body and its emotions.

When you think of how much energy you expend over the emotions, you will realize that you waste an awful lot of energy. That energy could be used in creating more energy in your *own* life to enable you to develop your Spiritual energy. Once you remove the emotions from the soul, there is a clear vision. One can see so much better, the past, the present and yes, the future.

The Higher Self has no emotions, it is the observer. It knows the right way. It knows the path you are to take. It has been directed with that path from before you were born. When you remove the emotions you become limitless because the Self has nothing to hold onto anymore. Let go of the emotions and the emotional body, and you can fly! That is how you can raise your vibration."

THE GRINDSTONE

"How many of you push the grindstone every day? By this I mean, how many of you go to your place of work and are thoroughly miserable at what you do? If this is you, then you need to step out of fear and into your dreams. So many of you

have dreams but do not believe that you can fulfil those dreams. Yet you can! You are capable, with the right thought, of being able to manifest all that you desire and more! You do this by eliminating *fear*. The fear of not having a job, the fear of not having enough money. There are so many fears, yet once they are removed, the barrier to manifesting comes tumbling down.

There are those who have been on the grindstone for decades, pushing the stone every day, hating each and every moment of it. Fearing change, fearing unemployment, fearing poverty, fearing so many things. Yet the Universe will provide all that you ask for, but you have to ask! There are those of you who ask and then in the next breath say, 'Oh, but that will never come my way,' or 'I do not deserve that,' or 'I am not worthy of such a thing.' While you do this, you will stay on the grindstone pushing the stone, and each year, it becomes heavier and heavier.

Try to stand outside the stone. Ask yourself, 'What would I like to do if I could do it?' Then start manifesting that reality. It may take some Earth time, but you will get there if you keep on being positive; not allowing anything negative to break up what you have created."

THE MAIN
LIFE LESSON

"The many religions of the world state that one should love *all* humanity, and there is nothing wrong with that statement. However, before one can love anyone else, one has to learn to love oneself. So many of you have a hatred for yourself. So many of you do not like who you are. Why is this?

135

It is because of many issues. Past life experiences, deep in the subconscious mind, are often at the root of these issues. Until they are removed, you keep attracting the same conditions over and over; it is as if you are running around in a circle whipping yourself. You say to yourself, 'Why do I keep having the same experiences? Why do I keep attracting the same kind of people?' You do this because you live the majority of your life in past life energy.

Within this energy lie the emotions of so many past incarnations. All you never expressed or released, is buried deep within your soul, waiting for the time it can be released, when you finally realize you want to let go of it. Some of it is buried so deep you have no idea it is there! It is only the energy of what you call God, who can help release that energy and enable you to move forward. Those experiences are like the layers of an onion, there are many layers. Each layer is like a raw wound, and once removed, needs Earth time to heal and recover before another layer can be removed.

The layers of unused energy stop the flow of Divine Love from the Creator. It is like being on the Earth plane without the Sun. Without the Sun there is no light, without the light there is dark. This light is the love that feeds you and assists in releasing the stored up past life energy. This energy also stops love from being experienced. Only when one can remove the layers of the onion, can one truly begin to love oneself! When the light enters the darkness, slowly, love can be experienced. Do not look outside of yourself for love, begin by loving yourself. When you can do this, you can truly love humanity!"

THE
MASTERS

"Over one hundred years ago, we, the Ascended Masters, contacted a Russian woman who was extremely intuitive and aware. This lady's name was Madame Blavatsky, and through the intuitive process we gave her the task of introducing us to the Earth plane. We felt it was the right time to introduce ourselves and to spread the word of us in the Spiritual realms, to the people.

Madame Blavatsky was guided to many religions, especially the eastern ones. From the Sanskrit writings of India and many other teachings, she became aware of the purpose of the Creator and of the future of humankind.

We asked her to make it simple, because her words were meant to be conveyed to the world. Most people in those days did not have a lot of learning, the upper echelons of society did, but the majority of souls did not.

Madame Blavatsky did try to make it simple, but got carried away with her communications with us, and with her inner feelings. She had a very strong Self which took control many times, changing the communications we gave her to suit itself. She smoked tobacco constantly which also stopped the messages from us from getting through clearly. Her aura was not clean with the constant smoking. She also became aware of the movement belonging to the Spiritual church and became very concerned that she would be likened to them.

We wanted to work with the churches. We saw the movement as a wonderful door to communication, but

137

Madame Blavatsky looked upon the church as fools and isolated herself from it. She was a headstrong woman, very strong and determined. The Self took command and what we had sent her to do, she did not do. She informed people that we lived in the Himalayas. She refused to accept that she herself was a Medium, and isolated herself even further from those who were mainstream Spiritual, creating a mystique for herself. She made many enemies and was not without a few tricks to surprise people. She became adept at magic, and manifested items to show the level of her skill.

While this was happening, we could only watch with sadness as our emissary twisted our words. She lied abominably about meeting us in the flesh, and wrote many words of untruth in her books. We were powerless to stop her. This incredibly gifted Medium, who we had hoped would take our words to the people, became more and more a recluse, and our purpose did not come to fruition.

She wrote books, but these books were so complicated that hardly any person could understand them. Our missive to her, that she made things simple so that people could understand her, fell on deaf ears. We never did get to the masses. Even today, her books are still not understood by many. What a waste of energy, and what a waste of talent.

When Madame Blavatsky died and returned to the Spiritual world, she was so upset when she saw what she had done. Like all souls, she had to see her whole life and its consequences before she could move on into her true home. She begged for a second chance; and so, it was decided that she would be given that chance and again return to the Earth plane with our message. This time she insisted she would get it right. To make sure that she did not get too 'heavy' and technical again, we made sure that she found it hard to use the left side of her brain. We made her more intuitive than she had been.

Since her passing into Spiritual realms, the society she founded, The Theosophical Society, has published thousands of books. All of them are based on or containing some of her information. They did not realize that the information was wrong.

The truth is this:
We, the Ascended Masters, *do not*, and *never have* lived in the Himalayas. We are in Spiritual realms and will remain here. We cannot live on the Earth plane either because our vibration is so high. We recruit disciples who agree before they come to the Earth plane, to work with us and these souls become our channels. To do this, they have to go through rigorous training to remove the Self and replace it with The Higher Self. This training consists of many years of discipline and hard work in learning to handle our energy, and also learning total obedience to us, so that *our* words, and *not* the channels are spoken.

There are many dimensions of the Spiritual world. We reside on one of the highest ones. We became Masters because we freed ourselves from the Earth plane. We repaid all of our karma and learned all of our lessons. Then, when we went into the higher worlds, we then worked our way up again in the many dimensions until we reached Ascension.

The world knows of only a few Masters, but there are thousands of us. We all work in the process of overseeing

139

the Universe and especially in trying to help humankind reach a higher state of being.

There are, what you would recognize as male and female energy Masters. The Lady Nada and the Lady Mary to name just two of the female energy Masters. Each one of us has a role to play in directing the energy of humankind on Earth to a higher vibration. We can only work through a channel, and this channel has to be specially trained. For those who are experienced in understanding astrology you can see, if you study *your* natal chart, if you are befitted to channel our energy.

Much has been written about we the Masters, but the majority of those words are not true. In time, humankind will recognize that what has been written in the past is not true. We wish it to be known that we are now ready, with Madame Blavatsky again, to take the word of us in Spiritual realms to the people. Madame has incarnated once again to be our channel, but this time to do it as we wish. This time, she has been an excellent student and is now ready to take our words to the world."

THE NEW MILLENNIUM

"What you know as the Aquarian Age is the time of new beginnings. For the new to come in though, the old has to change. Old ideas, old thoughts, they all have to go.

It is the purpose of the Ascended Masters to bring the new onto the Earth plane so that change may take place.

I have been asked many times in my channellings, 'Will there be an Earth plane after the year 2000 of Earth time?' Of course there will be an Earth plane, but it will be very different from the one you know now. In the last fifty Earth years, much change has already happened. The influence of the church with its narrow ways, and fear of God has started to change. There is an openness in relationships between the sexes, and many souls are searching for the Higher Self without the aid of religion or churches.

Humankind are now learning of the relationship between the body, mind and soul. It is very important that this is learned, because only when all three are in balance can a person find peace within themselves and have, 'a peace that passes all understanding.' Humankind are becoming aware of the meaning of reincarnation. In this incarnation you carry with you all of the lessons you have not learned in previous incarnations. For many souls they want free of that burden, which for some, feels like a weight around the shoulders or a noose around the neck. Eighty percent of this incarnation is affected by your previous incarnations. Everything that you do is also affected by your previous incarnation.

When you meet someone and do not like them, it is because your soul remembers something from a past incarnation where you were hurt by this person. When the opposite occurs and you meet someone you 'know' but do not know where from, this is because the soul remembers good times with that person.

You are not just a physical body. Each subtle body vibrates *141* at a different level. When they vibrate together as one, without conflict, then and only then, can you raise your vibration and move to a higher dimension.

What seems a lifetime to you on the Earth plane, is the blink of an eye to us in the Spiritual realms. There is no time, except what you have created on the Earth plane. The Earth plane is, and always has been, a plane of illusion. Only when you leave the body and return home to Spiritual realms can you see that illusion.

As more and more people decide to take back their own power and search for their truth and Higher Self, you will see a great deal of change taking place on the Earth plane. There will be changes too on a physical level, with weather conditions going against traditional patterns, Earthquakes and volcano eruptions.

This is the Earth plane preparing itself for the new millennium. Have no fear of the future, just be willing to accept the change and go with it. So many people fear change and yet it can set you free from old boring routines and open up new doors of excitement for people. Live in the *Now*, with no thought of anything but the *Now*, and there will be *no* fear. Each moment forward from the *Now* will then be a wonderful adventure."

Note: This was channelled at the start of the year 2000

THE NEW MILLENNIUM 2000

"Despite the fact that there is dissension over the date of the new millennium, humanity is coming to a very auspicious time in its history. The new millennium will bring forth many new souls searching for *their* truth and *their* Spirit. Many souls will decide that they no longer wish to remain on the Earth plane. For those souls who do decide to stay, much work needs to be done.

For those who profess to be Spiritual, I would ask that you try to forget your own needs and desires in the new millennium, and work for the good of humanity. The Self is always indignant when it has to do things it does not want to do. It is the perfect way to tame the Self by doing things for others, for humanity, for the Earth plane and not for oneself.

For those who profess to be Spiritual, know that, to be Spiritual one has to be completely in unconditional love. *Hatred of any kind is not of Spirit.*

For those who judge another, one day they too will be judged, for everything that goes out must return to its source.

Many unkind words are written to this website by those who profess to be Spiritual. No energy is given to these words and so they die, like the wind after a storm. For those souls, more than ever, they should question their Spiritual teachings, for all the Spiritual teachings speak of: *love, forgiveness and understanding another's views.*

I am not saying these souls are wrong, just that they have their own truth. Each man and woman should have his own, not that belonging to someone else. Even a husband and wife can, and should, be different. Only by finding peace in the soul, can one have peace in one's life. When humanity understands the Spiritual part of themselves, *143* *then* they will understand themselves. They will also have their own inner peace.

Finding peace in the soul involves going into many facets of the soul and discovering where the blocks lie. True Spiritual readers and healers can help one to do this. We the Masters, all of us, send to the Earth plane a ray of energy to help them create the new beginning that is required for humanity to find the peace it so desires. In the next ten Earth years, much of the old will be destroyed. Humanity has already decided where this will happen. There are no accidents, all has been decided on long ago. The new will rise like a Phoenix from the ashes.

From we, the Masters, we ask that all enlightened souls work hard to make the Earth plane a better place, to put the Self and its needs aside and work as brothers for the betterment of the World. Only then, will they feel the Spirit within them."

THE PAST

"Why do you live in the past?"

"Oh yes, I know it is necessary for your Spiritual development to know where you came from, but so many of you are in fear of the future, in fear of change. Life is a constant change, moving forward, learning, growing, becoming closer to the God force.

You cannot move forward Spiritually if you live in the past, in fear. What is there to fear about the future ahead of you? Why, it is a wonderful adventure. How wonderful to have the surprise of something new ahead of you. Have you forgotten that we are always with you, protecting you, guiding you and helping you? Do you not trust that we will lead you in the right direction? Think of what is to come as a wonderful adventure.

If you fear what is to come, then what you will get, is what you fear. Your future will always be fearful. If you look upon it as an adventure, then it will be a wonderful one. Like attracts like.

Many years ago, my channel faced change and she would not make the change, so the Universe placed her in a position where she had to change, she had no alternative. It became the best thing she ever did. It was the start of her learning that *all* change is wonderful. Let go of your fear, let go of your concern and just live in a positive perspective. *The past has gone, you cannot change it.* No matter what it did for you, you learned from it. Leave it there. Leave the past behind."

THE
PHYSICAL BODY

"Why do you have such a fascination with the body? It is just a vehicle, a carcass to carry the soul on this Earth plane. You are obsessed with the fact that your body is fat, or thin, or tall, or short. You spend hours discussing your body, its faults, its problems and why you don't like it. What a waste of energy!

You have the body that you need on this Earth plane. Some of you have the body you have because of Karma. Others, like my channel, have a large body to hold the energy needed. They are like batteries, holding the energy until it can be given to humanity. Others burn the

Spiritual energy and have difficulty in dealing with the energy.

There are those of you who deliberately bring back your food. You do this because you think you carry too much weight. There are others who do not eat and become so thin they often die. Each one of you has chosen your body. Yes, *you* have chosen it. You made the decision to have the body you have. When you stop the obsession with the body, with losing or gaining weight, when you accept that it is just a vehicle for the soul, then it will become like the sky above you and the Earth below you, just another illusion.

When you are concerned with your body, you waste energy which could be used elsewhere. Think about how much time you give to worrying about your body, your face, your hands, your feet, your hair, your ears, your nose, etc. How many hours have you spent doing this? Your body is the vehicle for your soul, for the Spiritual within, nothing more. Let go of your concerns for the physical form and you will then start to enjoy life. Your body too is an illusion."

The Problem of Becoming Spiritual Using Your Brain

by Dwjhal Kuhl – The Tibetan Master,
Guest of the Master Maitreya

"Really, a lot of problems in this area resolve down to almost a single issue, left brain versus right brain. As some people are aware the left part of the brain is the part that deals with 'logic and time'. It deals with looking at the past, evaluating it and then coming to a conclusion on the present or about the future. This looking at the past and working out what the future might be, can be anywhere from a few seconds to years. It is the mind or the Lower Mental Body of an individual. While the right side of the brain deals with the creative and Spiritual side of you where time is not involved. The right side of the brain handles inspiration coming in from the Higher Mental Body and above. Or to put it another way, handles information coming in from the highest planes of consciousness where Spirit reside. It's that simple!

The left side of the brain deals with the past and the future, while the right side deals only with the *Now*, this instant of time. The left side of the brain is restricted to conditioning in this life and past lives, while the right side of the brain has no such restrictions. It has access to all knowledge and wisdom. The left side is under the dominance of the *Self* or *Ego*, while the right side is connected to the *Higher Self*, the Spiritual and divine within you.

This left side of the brain is very useful in doing many

147

things that require systematic thought in the field of mathematics, cooking, programming computers, science and even driving a car. The left brain is very good at analyzing all sorts of things and coming to some conclusion as to the outcome of a set of conditions. These conclusions may be right or they may be wrong. Nevertheless, they are and can be very useful in day to day activities; only time tells.

The left brain, focused in the mind, is that part that allows humankind to identify with the physical plane and to realize that they are separate entities, with wishes, thoughts and desires. If these desires, wishes and thoughts are of a positive nature and do not interfere with another person's freewill, then all is fine, but this is most often not the case.

The left side is connected to the 'I am' part of people. The 'I am' part that says you want to do this, you want to do that and you do not want to get involved in anything you don't like or do not want to do. It is the selfish part of you!

Most of the decisions of the left brain revolve around 'pain and pleasure', usually on a short term basis. While the right side, connected as it is to the Higher Self, looks at a more a long term vision. This vision coming in from the Helpers, Guides, Teachers, and Masters from the plane of Spirit.

Meditation is a method of allowing you to shift your current left brain focus in day to day activities to the right brain, the creative and Spiritual where the Higher Self dominates and has a direct connection to the Divine. Think and ponder on these things and you will know that it is true."

Dwjhal Kuhl

THE PURPOSE
OF LIFE

" I have often been asked the purpose of life. The purpose of life is to grow in Spirit. Life is a school, an education. All those who come into your life are the teachers. Every soul acts as a mirror for you. Every soul is a teacher. From the beginning of your life you choose the conditions you require for your learning. Only you are responsible for what you choose. You then start your path through the grades of school, learning and growing.

Many souls complete their learning that they set up for themselves. Others fail, others achieve some of the learning. *You* are the only one who can help *you* to achieve the learning.

There is one barrier to you achieving your goal of learning and that is *Fear*. Fear is the worst energy you can have. It will stop you dead in your tracks. It will keep you a slave to your life lessons, stopping you from moving on.

The Master Jesus spoke of fear often in his teachings. If you have fear in your life then you have no growth, for the fear will stop you growing. Look your fear in the face, and see it for what it is – an illusion that you have created, and you will move forward and grow. It is not easy letting go of fear, but once it is faced, it becomes nothing, absolutely nothing! Why not face your fear?"

THE PURPOSE
OF THE SOUL

"I was asked the other day why there were no books written on Spiritual development. There are books in the world today on this subject, but many of the books are not read because the Self will do its best to stop you reading them. The purpose of the soul on the Earth plane is to grow. The soul has lived many incarnations and it is working to free itself from attachment, from desire, from greed, and all of the emotional ties which tie many of you to the Earth plane. It is about *Faith*, it is about *Trust*, it is about *Surrender* to a higher power. Yes, it is about letting go of the *Self*.

The Higher Self will always lead you to safety, and may I say, to a better life and better conditions. It does not want you to live in a negative way. It does not control either, but suggests the higher way. The Higher Self has all the answers, but the Self keeps getting in the way. The purpose of the soul is to conquer the Self, so that one may experience the peace and tranquillity of total love from the Divine, and with all that you need being manifested. There is no struggle, no fear, no desire, just a knowing that all that you need will be there. Often, this manifests as more than you desire. Doing this is not easy and the path is rocky and hard. For those who do it, they will find a wonderful way of life. They have the knowledge that there are no more incarnations; that their time on the Earth plane is finished."

THE SELF (Ego)
and the HIGHER SELF (Spiritual)

" *I* feel that this is the time now on the Earth plane, to educate souls about the Self. Until the Self is eradicated, the Earth plane cannot move forward. What is the Self and where did it come from? In order to explain this, I need to go back in Earth time, and warn you that this may be a long teaching.

There was once a planet in a far distant galaxy which had two Suns. It was a planet of great beauty and magnitude. The two Suns fuelled the energy for this planet and they were a very advanced civilization. It was a place of happiness, contentment and serenity. The souls in their evolution had evolved over many millenniums of what you on Earth would call 'time', into a race of Higher Self beings. They had the ability to leave their bodies and move to an even higher vibration if they wished to do so. They created a wonderful place, which many term 'Heaven' or the 'Spiritual World', where they could go and renew themselves when they needed rest and relaxation, or simply when they just needed change. This was looked after by a group of Spiritual beings called the Brotherhood; highly evolved beings with beautiful energy. They were known by the other members as 'The Masters.' These souls chose to stay in this place, and assisted in the organizing of life and pleasure on the planet with two Suns.

It does not matter the name of this planet, nor where it was in the galaxy. The purpose of this channelling is to explain about the Self.

One day it was noticed that both of the Suns were losing

energy, dying in other words. The Brotherhood were very concerned because they knew that without the Suns, they could not sustain their energy on a physical plane. Instructions were given to find another home. It was put to the beings on the planet that they could just go to the place of Spirit and stay there, but the souls on the planet enjoyed being in the physical, and so, word went out that a search was to be made for another 'home'. Space craft went out looking for this home, and after many searches in many places finally found the Earth plane.

At that stage of its development, the Earth plane was at a stage where the caveman was. Man had just evolved into the human shape but had little intelligence. The Brotherhood were elated to find this. It was decided that in order to connect with this race of beings, they would merge with this species through merging with the DNA and with cloning. This was done, and the new human was created and started to grow.

The new human being was more evolved than most of its kind, and as it grew, showed remarkable abilities which the normal caveman did not have. It was this new human who educated others about fire. Very soon the caveman began to evolve at a very quick rate. The new human soon bred with the old human, and the 'human' we know today was evolved.

The Brotherhood kept an eye on the new human beings and made regular visits to see if they were doing well. It is these early visits which are remarked on in the Christian Old Testament and described as Ezekiel Wheel and other

events. Scientists have often said they cannot find the missing link between caveman and the modern human, well this is it!

Soon though, they became aware that the new human being was different to those on the planet of two Suns. They started to fight, argue and became very negative. The Brotherhood were disturbed about this and were instructed to find out why this was happening. It was soon discovered that a mistake had been made. The new race of beings had the Higher Self of the Brotherhood beings, but they had also, through breeding, taken on the survival instinct of the caveman. It is this basic instinct type energy, which we now call the *Self*. This energy was only in the caveman. It was a natural energy designed to assist with survival. However it had been tampered with through breeding, and was now out of control. The Brotherhood realized that they had done a terrible thing, and started trying to put this right.

They decided that education was the answer. However, they could not cope with the numbers of human beings who were now multiplying and moving around the planet as well. It was decided to send messengers on a regular basis to assist with the teaching. Some Brothers chose to come and actually be born here to assist with that education. It is still going on today. Humanity has now come to a stage where a giant leap is about to take place. So many souls are now seeking their true Spiritual identity. Fifty Earth years ago, there were only a few searching, but now most of humanity is evolving beyond the Self. However, the Self is a formidable opponent and is fighting with all its might to stay in each human being.

In order for the Self to be eradicated, one needs to be in the energy of a highly trained channel and the energy of a Master. Only this energy will enable the transformation to take place. My channel has the training and she and I have started that work. It started in Perth, Western Australia, in October of the Earth year 2001. With Margaret, I became a keynote speaker. This enabled me to be the negative clearing house for many souls; for them, to make the transformation away from domination of the Self. The Photon Belt energy and Chiron, the 'healing' asteroid, which some call a planet, are also helping this cause. Once the Self is eradicated around the world, then the healing of the Earth plane can begin. This is the most important message that I have channelled for you. You cannot free the Self through normal means. Over the Earth years it has become a most formidable opponent.

The souls who came here originally, brought with them, the ability to return to the Spiritual world or Heaven, as many know it. However, this cannot happen while there are blemishes on the soul level, which have been created by the Self. Once these have been addressed and dealt with, souls will not come back to the Earth plane through reincarnation.

That is why the Master's course was created. It was created to assist souls in the freeing of the Self and moving onto the higher vibration; not to return to the Earth plane. To educate souls in understanding metaphysics and who they are on a Spiritual level. It gives the answers to why, how and what. But even there, the Self has its way, telling souls the course is too expensive, too far to travel, that the soul cannot take time off work, they are too old, etc, etc, etc. The Self will do anything to stop you moving on.

I have tried to explain this as clearly as I can, the channelling is not perfect because it happened such a long Earth time ago. We in the Spiritual realms do not live in the past, only in the now. The Self loves the past because there in all its glory are the excuses, emotions and feelings which it uses to imprison you. It really can be called the Devil and Satan. It has the ability to destroy you. Over thousands of Earth years, it has evolved and become very sophisticated, as you would say on the Earth plane, 'very crafty.' In order to survive and stay in the comfort zone, it will never stop in its efforts to stop you discovering and working with the Higher Self. For when you find the Higher Self, then you have the answers.

All of the prophets have been messengers of the Brotherhood. All of them moving humanity forward in evolution. Jesus taught so many wonderful things about fear. Mohammed taught new teachings, as did Buddha and all of the prophets of the past. In the last fifty Earth years there has been an influx of souls wanting to teach. It is the reason there has been so much teaching on the Spiritual. So many books written and so many people out in the world who are assisting us with the task of shifting the vibration of the Earth plane. It will be done. The light will come upon the Earth plane and the darkness will eventually pass. The Self will put up a battle, but there are so many souls with a desire for change into the Higher Self. If everyone had no fear, the task would be made easy. This is my teaching to you. Find out about your Self and become aware of it. Find a Spiritual healer who can assist you in finding where your Self is hiding, and where it is keeping you a prisoner. You will then be able to connect with your Higher Self."

THE SOUL

"What is the soul? The soul is the sum total of all you are. It is the past, present and future as you know it. It is the *Now!* The soul resides in your heart, not in your head. Your soul feels, breathes and lives while in your Earthly body as a part of you. You are body, mind and soul. The Spiritual part of you is the soul.

It is each soul's purpose, very like the sperm trying to find the egg, to strive in this incarnation for growth, freedom from the Earth plane and the continuing round of existence it continually endures. The soul will lead you to teachers, books and all sorts of ways of freeing yourself from the Earth. Often you do not listen. You do not listen because you fear change, fear looking at yourself, which is a very important part of moving forward.

You see, you have a Self. It is attached to the Earth plane, and does not want to see you ascend; nor does it want you to grow. The Self will do everything in its power to stop the Soul from growing. You, the body and mind, are usually unaware of this. That is the soul. Look to your heart, not your head. It is not of logic, but of the heart. It feels it is the *true* part of you; the part you will return with to the Spiritual realms. Find the Soul and you will have found the most wonderful part of you. Logic will tie you up in knots with explanation."

THEOSOPHY

"I have been asked many times about the subject of Theosophy. Do I support it, am I a part of it?

The answer to that is yes and no. Yes, because it is part of many belief systems in the world today for those who believe in this way of studying the Spiritual. Yes, I support it because for those souls who are searching and find Theosophy, it *can* be, for them, a door opening onto a wider world.

The answer no, is also relevant. It is so, because, for those souls who do not wish to be attached to Theosophy, who find it difficult to understand the Indian words and the way of Theosophy, I offer them something different; the teachings in a very simple form.

Many souls do not want to be involved in churches, organizations, religions and Spiritual groups. They wish to serve the Spiritual realms alone. My writings are for them. Many have said they find Theosophy very difficult to understand. For those people I open another door. Many souls get great upliftment and Spirituality from Theosophy. However, there are souls who do not want to be involved with that concept.

If one is truly Spiritual then one can accept *all* thoughts on the Spiritual; choosing to take what one needs. For those who are Spiritual and who find it difficult to understand why there are so many different views on the Spiritual, I would answer this by saying to you, 'There are many different souls on the Earth plane today. Each soul has its own vibration, as does the word of the Spiritual.

157

Even those who study Christianity are in the right too. There is room on the Earth plane for *all* views. Those souls who are searching, will find the view that suits them. They should be allowed to do so."

THOUGHT ENERGY

"very thought becomes something, from the moment of its conception, the thought becomes reality. Every time you think, whether *good* or *bad* thought, you immediately set up a reality. Once you create a thought, about something or someone, that thought is destined to manifest. If it does not, it goes back within. But it does not go back to where it came from, because it has been created and cannot be uncreated. So it goes within the Etheric (Auric body) and stays there, unmoving, still, waiting until it can be used.

If it is not used, which is usually the case, then it becomes stagnant negative energy. This negative energy permeates the Auric body and eventually, because it is not going anywhere, becomes stagnant matter. This then travels to a part of the body, and usually, because it is Etheric, gathers in the chakras and starts to affect the physical body.

Often, you will have a thought about someone. You feel you want to communicate something, but do not do this. You then set up an energy (thought) block in the throat Chakra. Perhaps you are frightened to open the door to the Spiritual part of you. You think about this but do not do it; you then create an energy (thought) block in the third eye or crown Chakra, to give an example of just two areas of blockage.

Over Earth time, and often many incarnations, because it cannot be seen, it stays there becoming more and more angry because it cannot move. You have stopped it by not acting and allowing the creation of the energy to flow. It then turns inwards *trying* to get back to its Creator. It cannot do this because it is not possible. It is of the Spiritual, not the physical and it needs a Spiritual channel to remove it. It has been created. You cannot de-create it, except by Spiritual healing, or divine intervention of some sort such as prayer. *All* thought is energy, and *all* energy has to move forward. Just as the human sperm has only one purpose and that is to fertilize the female, so energy as thought has only one purpose, and that is to create what has been thought. Negative thoughts will create negative realities, positive thoughts will create positive realities. That is how blockages are created.

Only the divine energy of the Spiritual realms can clear these blocks. Through your own bringing in of that energy (if you are not too heavily blocked with this energy), or through someone else, such as a healer, the power of the Spiritual energy can, if there is the right channel for that energy, shift the block of energy and dissipate it until it does, in fact, return to where it came from i.e. universal energy.

Removing this stagnant, negative energy, then allows the Spiritual body to vibrate at a higher rate of vibration."

TIME

"From childhood, time and space are considered by the way in which we are taught by parents, surroundings, and most of all, conditioning. There really is no time, or space, only our concept of it. Once again, placed in the mind by past experiences. When conditioning is removed, when we no longer consider what we have been taught in the past as *fact*, then we allow ourselves to be free to create our own time and space. The Universe is free of time and space, there is only the *Now*, and so, no restrictions are placed on the planets, stars and solar systems. All is *Now!*

If we allow conditioning to leave our lives, we find for instance, that the body, free of having to respond to a clock or to restriction, is suddenly free to be its own master, and so, will start to operate free of conditioning. The natural rhythm of the body, that part of us that when we were born was pure, untainted by life on Earth, will once again become pure and untainted. It will start to operate as it should, naturally, without force and in balance with nature. Our concept of the soul is one of a Spiritual appendage attached to the body, when in fact, the soul is a part of the Universe. It has been there from the beginning and will be there for evermore. The body is only a receptacle for that universal energy. The body changes each incarnation or lifetime.

Because space is unlimited and unrestricted, we can if we wish, travel forwards or backwards in time. We can choose the lifetimes we wish to have incarnations in. Our thinking is that if we die in say 1995, then we can if we wish return again in the year 2000. The mind accepts this because this is what we have been taught. It is however, a misconception. Yes, we can die in 1995, but it is possible if we wish to return for another lifetime in 1940, 1910, or even in the 1800, 1700 or even before.

When you leave the concept of time behind, then you become incredibly mediumistic and aware intuitively. For many this concept is difficult to understand and many do not even want to accept it. Many are ready to accept it, and for those, it will open a new door to thinking."

Channelled in 1994

TIME FOR CHANGE

"For many thousands of Earth years, the Creator, God, or the Divine Soul if you wish to give it a name, has sent many prophets to the Earth plane who have brought change with their teachings and with their words of wisdom. Earth History is filled with such people, Jesus, Mohammed, to name just two. Their purpose has been to bring to the Earth plane the teachings necessary for humankind to change their vibration, and enable them to raise their consciousness.

Each prophet or messenger has created a following, and each following has created division within its members. In the Christian faith, for instance, it has led to many churches, faiths and groups, all claiming to have the right answer, and to be *the testimony* to the teachings.

The time has come for humankind to become their own Master. To leave behind the teachings of the past, many of

161

which have led to war around the world, and to become its own Master. To show no allegiance to any human form but, 'To itself be true.'

Humankind is now ready to leave behind allegiance to any particular group, prophet or person, and the New Age will enable them to truly become divine themselves. It is bringing the teaching of communication with Spiritual realms, astrology, time and space, channelling and many other subjects. Once humankind has the knowledge of these matters, then they will be able to free themselves of all ties to other sources of information. They will have direct communication with the Higher Self and with the Creator.

When one shows allegiance to any particular group, then one becomes a slave to that source, believing *that* belief and not finding answers for oneself. In the future, all humankind will, if they wish, be able to find their own answers and to become their own Masters.

Only then, can humankind break away from bondage, war, and will peace be upon the Earth plane. When humankind no longer follows like sheep and follows their own thoughts and divine inspiration, truly then will they be divine. Then, those of the Spiritual realms will speak through them and to them individually."

TITHING

"I am often asked about tithing, which is the giving of a portion of one's earnings or energy to help others.

'Do you approve of this?' I am asked. Yes, I do approve of this action.

When you give away a portion of what you own, this then makes way for more to come in. The Universe will bring a constant flow, but it is when you hold on to what you have, that you stop that flow. The portion you give can be five percent, or fifty percent, but by giving, you are creating the energy of more.

Once you start giving, the Universe says, 'Oh, this person has not got enough, we will bring in more,' and this is exactly what happens. It may not come in the form of money, it may come in the form of gifts or something you need, but the Universe knows that all has to be balanced and as you give away, so it comes back.

You have to give away with love though, not for what you will get back. If you give away because of what you will get back, the purpose behind the giving is wrong. When one opens the heart and gives, then the Universe will know this from the action of love. Your life will change once you start this process.

There are many organizations which can benefit from tithing, from giving your portion to help build wells so that villagers in poor countries can have a ready supply of water, to giving to help the work done by those such as this site. *You* will know when you come to do it, where your portion shall go.

Listen to your heart, look around you to see where you can help. Do not stop another soul from growing by helping individuals, but help to further the work of those organizations who need it."

TOUCHING AND PERSONAL CONTACT

"So many of you do not have personal contact. Your skin or body is never touched by another, yet the body craves being touched, hugged, held and loved. The majority of you have become so conditioned to *not* allowing anyone into your space that you have forgotten the feeling of being touched.

One can touch another without being sexual. One can touch another without there being an intention behind it. Touch is the most important part of life; being touched by another, whether in a massage, by a partner or friend. It is *so* necessary that you learn to touch each other.

Until you can learn to let go of any inhibitions or fears pertaining to personal contact and touching another, then you cannot move forward on your path in life. You stay stagnant like a pool of stale water, unmoving; the energy inside of you still and dead.

Touch is a part of the initiation process of Spiritual development. When you allow another to touch you, you open up your heart Chakra, then emotion and feeling can be experienced. Whether in friendship, love or sexual contact, it is a fundamental part of living and it connects with the energy of your body.

A person who is not touched is like a flower without water. The flower calls out for water to all who pass, but nobody waters it. That is what your body does all the time. It cries out to be touched and yet you deny it, either through fear, because you fear being hurt, or you feel it is wrong to touch another, especially one of the same sex!

A person who is touched on a regular basis either through personal touch, through love, sexual contact, a massage, or even by a friend with regular hugs, is a person who glows and who feels alive. For they have fed their soul, by allowing that personal contact.

Know that the path to Mastership is not one of austerity, hardship or pain, it is simply letting go and feeding the soul of what it desires on a Spiritual level. All aspirants to Mastership have to let go of their fears of personal contact and allow themselves to touch and to be touched. Then does the soul know contentment.

Feed the body care and concern through touch, and you are feeding the soul."

TRANSPLANTED BODY ORGANS

"One of the many questions asked of me is about body organ transplants. 'What is the Spiritual world's view?' Well, our view is simple. It is a necessary part of life and will continue to be so.

The person who requires the body organ, such as a heart or a liver, has brought the condition with them from a previous lifetime. Usually with the liver there has been anger, resentment and frustration in past lives. The soul has not cleared this from their soul memory, and so, another soul who owes that person karma, or who offers to help the soul, chooses to come to the Earth plane and live a short life in order to help by donation; to give a new

165

organ to that soul. Whenever there is illness, there is a soul searching. The soul really looks at *their* life. It gives them a chance to really look death in the face and this then creates the healing crisis, or shift in consciousness, necessary to move on spiritually.

The soul who passes to the Spiritual realms learns many lessons through the act of donation and so too the soul who needs the organ donation. Sometimes, an organ transplant takes place and the soul receiving the transplant chooses to die. When this happens, it is their choice, perhaps they do not want to continue with their life path. Perhaps the changes internally and on a Spiritual level are too much for them. It is their choice to leave the Earth plane, but they will still, in some incarnation, have this in their karmic record and will have to return to experience the situation again. That is the Law of Karma.

One thing is certain, and that is, that the soul receiving the organ donation is never the same after the experience. Their lives change and they learn to appreciate every moment of every day. They do not waste a second of Earth time.

There will be more of this happening in the future as scientists and the medical profession grow organs to help supplement the need for transplanted organs. There will, one day, be no need for this because in Earth time, humanity will realize eventually, the real cause of illness and disease. That time is not too far away. Until that day happens though, the need for transplanted organs will be there. While it is there it will be a tool of learning for all souls involved."

TRUST

" or each soul on the Earth plane, all that they need can be provided; they just have to learn to trust, to let go of fear, doubt, insecurity and other such negative energies. Those feelings are brought through from other incarnations; they have not been cleared from the soul memory and they wreak havoc on the life of those who experience them.

Ask of yourself, why do I fear? Does it come from an experience in this incarnation? If it does, then speak with a Spiritual advisor and clear it from the soul memory. If you know it does not come from this incarnation, then seek a Spiritual person who can help you access a previous one, where it originally came from. Fear is energy that has been trapped. It was once a thought that became negative, because of an experience that was unpleasant and not understood. Once it is found it can be released, never to haunt the soul again.

The Creator, God as many call this energy, Divine Soul as some others call it, or whatever name you may give to this Energy, cannot work through you if you have fear; for it is negative energy and it blocks the flow of positive energy coming in. All that you need can be there. Your every need can be supplied if only you will stop the worry, fear, doubt and other negative emotions. Once they are removed, then the Creator can send to you all that is due yours.

Often you are not aware of your negative issues. It is only when one visits a Spiritual healer/teacher/counsellor that

167

one can find out where ones blocks are. Once one has removed the blocks, the energy can flow uninterrupted. If one then trusts and *knows* that all that one needs will be provided, no soul need go hungry, be poor or be without. Each time you say to yourself, 'I will never be rich,' you create that energy. It is a negative statement. Remove it and replace it with a positive one of, 'I will be rich and when I am, I will use my money for good works as well as use the money for myself.'

There is nothing wrong with abundance if one tithes a portion of it. When one tithes, then one keeps the energy flowing. There is a presumption that to be Spiritual one has to be poor. This is from the days when this did occur, it no longer applies. All souls should have abundance, what they need can be provided and more if they wish as long as they use the energy wisely.

Trust is letting go of all the negative and allowing the Divine energy of the Creator to fill your life and bring to you the happiness, success, financial reward that is yours by right. Each soul has the ability to create all they need, they just have to trust, let go and then fly! You will be amazed at how far you can go."

TRUTH

"The subject of truth is very interesting because it asks many questions. For instance, what is truth? Just the word, truth, can have a different meaning in every dictionary that you have. To be truthful means not to tell a lie, and yet what is a lie? A lie can be one man's truth. This may sound like a Chinese puzzle but it raises quite an issue that humankind, on Earth, have not considered and that is the meaning of truth.

Each person has their own truth. My channel Margaret's truth is hers alone and may differ from that of her partner. If this is so, then who is correct? Both are, because they both see truth, but in their own way. It is more important to be honest than to be truthful because when one is honest, one is true to oneself. Each one of you on the Earth plane can look at a picture on a wall, and each one of you will see a different picture to another person. One may see the same picture and comment that the light in the picture is too intense. Another may comment on the darkness of the shadows, or the colours of the oils not being correct. Each of you sees the picture as *you* see it, not as anyone else sees it and there is the difference.

No human on Earth can profess to know the truth, because one man or woman's truth can be another's folly. No one person can be correct at any time, because they are correct only as *they* see it, not as another person sees it. If another person agrees with that truth then it is good, but it is not wrong to see something different. If you insist on a person taking your truth, then you impinge on their freewill. They have to see the subject for themselves and make their own decisions. The decision may be not to accept your truth. You have become sheep on the Earth plane, not wanting to follow your own truth, but taking another's truth as your own!

169

It is our intention with the higher vibration of energy entering the Earth plane, to enable you to start becoming your own person. To see your own truth, even though another may not believe that, it is *your* truth. When one accepts another's truth, one then cuts oneself off from the intuitive process and also from one's *own* truth. When one accepts one's own truth, then you become the individual that you are supposed to be.

So much argument and war is started over one person insisting on his or her truth! How many times have you caused grief with your friends and family because you insisted on your truth? Why can you not accept that you are all individual vibrations? Each one of you is separate from the other, even identical twins are not the same, but have different personalities and vibrations. Once you accept your own truth and acknowledge another's as their own, without argument or dissension, then you become enlightened, because you raise yourself above the sheep. Only by doing this, and being detached from another's truth, can one truly change the Earth."

UPDATE ON
THE PHOTON BELT

"Since I wrote the channelled article on the Photon Belt a few years of Earth time ago, much has happened in the world. Humanity is finally starting to look at itself and is seeing the wrong it has done the planet. More and more souls are searching for the Spirit within; for some, it is as if they are running out of time.

The energy of the Photon Belt has started working around the Earth plane. Souls are leaving in huge numbers, and the Earth plane is changing and cleansing itself.

There has been so much doom and gloom and negative predictions about the future of the Earth plane. I want you to know that all is as it should be.

The Spiritual work is progressing. Do not have any fear about the future of the Earth plane. She has a wonderful future, and hopefully, if you have no fear, you will be a part of it."

VIRUSES

"There is much misunderstanding about the role of the virus and the Spiritual person. It is often thought that if one has raised one's vibration spiritually, then one should not get ill or contract viruses. This thinking is wrong.

When a person has raised their vibration, they have done so in the Spiritual body. However, the physical body is still the same way it has always been. Because of the raised vibration and the change in energy the body may look younger. If the person follows a good diet and has the right state of mind then it will show in the physical, but basically the physical body is the same as it always has been. It is a vehicle for the Spiritual.

When a person contracts a virus, whether it be, what is known as 'the flu' or something more serious like HIV/AIDS, they have chosen to do so. Some people choose a virus to make their exit from the Earth plane. Others choose it to help them clear blocks and deeply hidden conditions from their physical bodies such as

171

childhood trauma, or past life conditions that have been carried over.

This also explains why in a crowd of people some people get viruses and others do not. Often a wife will get a virus and be quite ill and yet her husband or partner will never get it.

It may surprise you to know that there is nothing 'evil' in the world, everything is perfect, and everything works in perfect order. You attract to you what you need to learn from, and to help you heal. You can also make your suffering easy or hard. You make the choice.

Many have contracted the AIDS virus and not died, and yet others have because they chose to die. This is how they make their transition into the Spiritual realms. Those that live, usually make a significant turn-around with their lives. Not only have they changed their own lives, but also, they have changed the lives of many around them.

Do not fear viruses. They come not as enemies, but as friends to help you, either in transition, or to heal in some way."

WAR

"There is so much fighting on the Earth plane. Man against man, brother against brother, faith against faith. We in Spirit are so powerless to help humanity with this problem except through the writings we channel and the messages we speak through those channels. To do so would interfere with the freewill of humanity.

You have often said, 'Why does God not stop this fighting?' Yet, it is not God who does this, but yourselves. The recent mass evacuation in Kosovo has been repeated before many times, like with Moses thousands of years ago. Yet humanity is still following the same pattern thousands of Earth years later.

Why does humanity fight? It does so because it is filled with fear. The fear of someone taking what is theirs; humanity wanting domination over others, yet there is enough for all on the Earth plane. You are all capable of manifesting everything you need.

Until humanity understands the Spiritual part of themselves, they will continue to have war. Not the Spiritual part of themselves that is taught in schools or by other faiths, but the real reason for their visit to the Earth plane as a soul. For many, the fighting has been an ongoing situation, incarnation after incarnation. Like your computer programmes today, if the program is not changed, it stays the same. So humanity en masse, needs to change the programming. If each soul were in touch with their soul, they would be able to do this.

It is our intention to reach out to as many souls as possible and help to change the programming of humanity. Only then, will there be peace."

WEIGHT LOSS

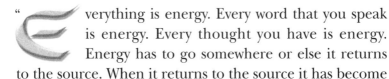 verything is energy. Every word that you speak is energy. Every thought you have is energy. Energy has to go somewhere or else it returns to the source. When it returns to the source it has become

changed because of the thought that was attached to it. For instance, positive thoughts go out and are used; positive words that are spoken create more positive energy. They motivate, create, empower.

Negative thoughts do one of two things, they either create fear, doubt, insecurity or any other negative emotion, or they go back in. Because they have not been used, they return to the source as energy, unused energy that just becomes stagnant. Negative words have the same effect.

When a person has no motivation, has a low opinion of themselves, has fear or doubt about anything, they create negative energy. If they speak negative words, those words destroy, create fear, doubt and insecurity in those they are aimed at. This creates blocks in the Spiritual body, namely the Chakras, which in turn affects the physical component of that, which is the glands. When the glands are not functioning properly, the body does not function properly because energy is blocked and cannot go where it has to go. The Spiritual body and the physical body are one, not separate as has always been thought. The physical, the emotional, the mental and the Spiritual bodies all work as one *together*, not separate to each other. When they are in balance, the whole body is in balance. If one body is out of synchronicity, this affects the flow of energy and usually that energy goes within, back to the source.

People who have a weight problem, who are either, overweight, underweight, anorexic or bulimic have this problem because they do not allow the energy to flow. These people are nearly always insecure, or have fear, or some other negative emotion. This problem can also be brought through incarnation after incarnation; compounding, life after life, like a Danish Layer cake, layer after layer after layer.

It is not the weight that is the problem. It is the cause of the weight and where it came from originally that is the problem. When the cause of that is found, the person usually loses the weight, never to put it on again.

It is not the calories you eat, as you humans call them, but the fact that you eat to provide sweetness in your life. You eat to comfort yourself at times of fear, doubt or insecurity. When you find the course of that doubt, fear and insecurity, you then no longer need to eat the way you did.

It is usually the case that those who have a weight problem have no motivation for exercise. They do not like being seen because of their weight, so another scenario is created; that of the overweight person *not* exercising because they cannot motivate themselves. It is a vicious circle.

Those who work with weight loss as a profession have only part of the answer. The answer lies in the energy and the fact that energy must go somewhere. Once it is spoken or thought, it has to be created. If it is not created it returns to the source. When it returns to the source, it is changed. If it was positive it can help the physical body through the glandular system to be well, just like positive energy through the hands of a healer or therapist. If it is negative, it blocks the glandular system and creates disease, or disease.

Find the cause of your problem and you will find the answer to your weight gain; but also look at past life conditioning. Many souls find the solution to their *175* problems from this incarnation, but if the problem is not cleared on a Spiritual level through past life or incarnation therapy, the problem will return. You need to get to the original source and then it will be no more, ever!"

WHAT ARE ANIMALS?

" I have been asked many times about animals and their role on the Earth plane. I must say though that many will disagree with what I discuss here. However, it is truth. I have discussed animals before in my channelling on animals and karma, and one on your animals taking on your conditions.

Animals are part of evolution too, they are souls just like you are. However, they are different in that they live in the *Now.* Whereas, you live in the past for most of your life and you worry about the future. Animals do not do this. By living in the *Now,* they do not have the past, nor do they concern themselves with the future. All they are concerned with is their survival now. They can be trained to be almost human, and yes, with repetition, they can understand your language. They know the words 'food' and 'walk' and many other words. They soon adjust to your thinking, and know that the more they love you, the more you will love them.

My channel Margaret was concerned at placing her cat in a cattery while she went to New Zealand for a month. I assured her, not only will the cat get good care by people who specialize in cats, but the cat will live in a state of *Now.* Although it may be a month of Earth time to Margaret, to the cat, there will just be the *Now.* There will be no timeframe for the cat. Yes, the cat may miss her, but soon, it will settle down and before it knows it, Margaret will be home.

I have been asked, 'Do animals become humans?' Yes of course they do! They evolve just as you evolved. Each incarnation they become closer to human. Usually, when they become human, they are born into tribal communities where they learn to be human. They then evolve from there.

Margaret once asked me where a certain fear came from and I showed her a life where she was a dog. The recall in Margaret was incredible, she could see it all. She never doubted after that experience.

Animals can become the most wonderful of companions, friends and even family. Many of you have had incarnations in many lives with your animals, hence the closeness you felt when you met your animal. More than anything, animals are a part of humanity, a part of Spirit. Yes, they do go into a group soul, similar to a tribe. But when they wish to visit you, or you wish to visit them in Spirit, this is made possible and you meet individually. Their love for you transcends all of time as you know it.

There are a few who mistreat their animals, and I have been asked, 'What happens to these souls?' I can assure you, when these souls see themselves in the Hall of Mirrors, without the Self there, they are mortified! And so, what goes out must come back in another incarnation. They will not come back as an animal, despite what certain Buddhists say, but they will experience ill treatment exactly in measure to what they gave out in this life. It is the rule of the Universe, what you give out, you get back!

177

Love your animals, for they love you – unconditionally."

WHAT DO I THINK
OF RELIGION?

"One question that I am often asked is what I think of religion, especially of those who are Christian, Jewish or Moslem. It is a question that raises itself very often. My answer is always that if a soul seeks God the Divine Being, the person should be free to do so in any way they feel they need.

There is only one God, Divine Being or Creator. How you communicate with that Energy is your choice. Some choose a religion, some choose to be alone. It does not matter how you communicate. All paths lead to God or this Higher Energy if you do not call it God.

There are those on the Earth plane who believe that they know the answers and are in communication with God. They believe they have a right to force people to believe in one way of communication. But if you try to force a child to eat a vegetable it does not like, the child will rebel. It will fight, it will show its dislike. It is the same in the older person. When you do not like something, you cannot enjoy it, nor can you believe it. This creates conflict in your being. The Earth plane is a large planet, there is room upon it for many different faiths and belief systems, and each soul, if it is allowed, will find its own path to God or the energy known as that.

On this website a few Earth years ago, I wrote a teaching on Truth, in which I said that each man or woman has their own truth. That one person's truth is another person's folly. I reiterate this with a person's belief in a higher energy. Each soul has their own way of finding their higher energy and the way they communicate with it. It is only when it is interfered with that anarchy follows. A soul should be able to communicate with the higher energy in their own way. It is a personal choice. If people did not interfere with this choice, the world would be a more peaceful planet. If you criticize another for their belief, you are criticizing yourself, for no soul has the truth of the planet, only their own truth."

WHAT DO WE DO?

" I have often been asked, 'Master, why do we need Spiritual Guardians, Guides and Masters?'

Well, you need them because without them, you would not be able to move forward spiritually. Our role with you is to move you forward, to place you in the situations you need to learn from; provide the intuition which will help to manifest this.

Can you imagine our dismay when we have spent a lot of energy getting you to a point where you can finally repay your karma, or make peace with an adversary, or repay a debt, which in Spirit, you have chosen to do before you were born, and you run away?

Oh, the dismay I can tell you! We work so hard in our dimensions to enable you to grow.

We know that *you* make choices, but a lot of energy is spent on you. Your Guardians and your Guides take you through the first stages of your development. They prepare you for the energy of a Master. When you are

179

ready, and this takes for you much Earth time and personal development, then a Master joins with your energy and you can truly begin your Spiritual work. That is the purpose of these souls. It is as simple as that. There is nothing complicated about it.

We, the Masters, will not channel through you until you have proved your worth. This involves letting go of so many things. Letting go of the comfort zone and learning to do things Spirit's way. Letting go and allowing Spirit to work with you, not trying to do it yourself. It is a surrender towards the Higher Self. We will never harm or hurt you neither will we manipulate you. We just wish to work with you.

It can take as long as twenty Earth years before you are fully ready to accept a Master.

All souls can do this, no matter how they enter the world, poor, rich, black or white, all are capable of union with a Master."

WHAT HAPPENS WHEN YOU PRAY? (1)

"Many millions of people pray every day, yet many of you do not know what happens when you do this. First of all, let me explain you need to ask to receive. This is very important. You cannot assume we know what you need. We only know when you ask. Until you speak it, only then, can we begin to work on it.

As an example, what if you ask for help to pass your

exams! Well, we can do this, but only if you put the right amount of energy into it. If you do not do the work in study, or if you have too many other things which take precedence over that study, then we cannot assist you. I have said often there are no magic wands. Everything is determined on how much energy *you* put into the subject involved.

There are those who pray for the life of a loved one. If it is the person's destiny or choice to leave the Earth plane and return back to Spirit, then it is *their* choice. There is nothing we can do, nothing can change that. We can however, help them with their transition over.

What of those who ask for assistance with the healing of their body, mind and Spirit? We hear your prayers as we hear all of your prayers. However, if the mind is set in unbelief in Spiritual energy, again, we can send the energy, but if it is not used it does not go to waste, but it cannot do the work it is supposed to do.

We do listen to your prayers, oh yes! Each one of you who has prayed or is praying, we hear you; but you must be aware of what happens on our side. Believe me; it is so sad to see the energy we send to you not being used because of your busy lifestyle or your disbelief in Spirit. Even a small belief will start the healing process. Yes, there are those who have no belief and who get well again. This is because although consciously they do not believe, usually because of family or outside pressure, on a subconscious level they do, but cannot tell anyone. There is so much to prayer, not just the act of you saying it."

WHAT HAPPENS
WHEN YOU PRAY? (11)

"When you pray, every prayer is heard, never doubt that. The Ultimate Being whom many know as God, hears every plea and every request. Your Guardian Spirit is then instructed to do whatever they can to assist.

In this second part of the writing on prayer, let us discuss what happens if you pray for an item, such as the need to find a particular book or for money to assist you. Your Guardian Spirit takes control of this and asks his or her Helpers to assist with providing what you need. However, astrologically this may not be possible.

For instance, you ask for assistance financially. You may, at the time of asking, have something in your astrological chart, which inhibits abundance coming to you at that moment of time. There may be something you have to learn from all this. If there is the wrong planetary energy, this can temporarily halt the supply. Your Guardian will await the passing of this transit or transits until there is a more positive outcome astrologically. This can be why your requests are not answered immediately.

If you put out your request and then have the faith and the belief to know it will come, it will come. However, if you say, 'I prayed, but nothing happened, so I do not believe,' and continue to have that belief, you will stop the flow of energy when it can come.

Sometimes your Guardian and Helpers cannot assist you when you ask, but it will come in time. Many of you pray and then, when the prayer is, as you think, 'not heard,' you disbelieve and actually stop the flow for the future.

Of course, your own subconscious mindset can also be an inhibitor to prayer. If on a subconscious level you have a belief you will not do well, do not deserve abundance, cannot achieve what you desire, then this is what you will have in your life. It pains us on our side of Spirit to see many of you not having the opportunities you deserve, because of your subconscious programming.

When you pray, understand that it may take some Earth time to bring what you desire into your energy. Much work is done in our space to make sure that eventually, you get what you request. *You* are often the one who stops that flow of energy."

WHAT HAPPENS WHEN YOU PRAY? (111)

"And so my final writing on prayer! What happens if you ask for a personal item, such as a special book or to find a teacher? This is where the Guides and Helpers who assist your Guardian Spirit come into play. Your Guardian has a whole array of souls who are waiting to work and assist in any way they can.

Once the request is made, then scouts are sent out looking for what is required. As you can understand, this can take some Earth time, but it will manifest. Sometimes an item can be transported from one space to another. This does not happen often because it takes an enormous amount of energy, but it can be done.

183

When the item is found, say for instance you have asked for a special book. Then in your sleep state, you will be told where to find it. When you wake and over the next few Earth days, you will have the 'feeling' to go to a certain place, or to contact a certain person, and on doing so, find what you are looking for. You may open a book and the answer to your question may be there.

You may have someone come into your energy who can provide you with what you need. We work very hard to obtain it for you. Sometimes, it can be many years before an item is found. My channel made a request many years ago for a certain book. It was a rare Spiritual book, but although it took three Earth years, we managed to find one for her and she is now the owner of that item. We do all we can to manifest your wishes and desires. If it is of the Earth plane, we can provide it eventually.

There is more to prayer than many think. I still have not covered all of the aspects of it, but hopefully have given you an insight into what happens when you pray."

WHAT IS LOVE?

"What is Love? Love is looking at another and seeing the beauty in them. It is having compassion and understanding for all living things. It is being non-judgmental, accepting the other soul for what they are; seeing the divine inside of them despite their Earthly impediments. Love does not want to interfere, nor does it want to stop another from growing. Yet it gently helps, making suggestions if asked, allowing the other soul to find their *own* answers in their *own* way. Love does not want to control, nor does it want to dictate.

Love does not give energy to anything. It just allows the flow of life to pass it by, understanding the times when sometimes things do not go perfectly. At these times, love is really strong and, if allowed, can conquer the darkness that accompanies such times. Love has no judgment of another. It recognizes that each soul has their own path and their own plan for their life. It does not see imperfection. Love can see into the soul and understand why the soul has that path to take. When one can achieve all of the above, then one can merge with God, the Ultimate Being, and can become at one with that Energy. That then is true bliss, Nirvana, Heaven. That is what Love is!"

WHO is GOD?

"Who is God? God is not a person, soul, or being. God is Energy, pure Love. It is the highest energy of the Universe. It is not tainted by negative thoughts. It is pure consciousness of the Higher Self in each and every one of you. It is a force to be used for your own growth and expansion. This force is not judgmental, it understands that each soul has its own lessons and level of learning. It is neither a Father nor a Mother waiting to scold. Nor is it the God that many people say one has to Fear. When humankind finally reaches the energy of this being, it is so exquisite that nobody has ever been able to describe it.

185

This energy is within *you*, each one of you, waiting to be

turned on to be used for the betterment of humanity. However, the Self, the fear, doubt, insecurity, and all other negative emotions, known by many as 'The Devil' or 'Satan,' will do everything in its power to stop you attaining the bliss of union with the energy of the Higher Self.

If you attest to be a Spiritual person, if you are on the Spiritual path, you will hate no soul, despise no soul. There will only be love in your heart for other souls, no matter what circumstances they may be in or going through, or may be doing to you.

This force of energy known as God is all knowledge and wisdom. When you merge with this energy you have what St Paul described in Corinthians in the Christian Bible as, 'the gift of all knowledge.'

Each soul in this lifetime can attain that communion. Each soul can feel the energy and the love of that force. You can do that by simply having no connection to anything negative and to letting disharmony in your life go, by not seeking revenge or hatred. By practising love in all that you do. When you can do that, you will then know the energy known by many as God."

WHY DO I ONLY SPEAK ENGLISH?

"I have been asked many times, 'Master, why if you are the World Teacher, do you not speak all the languages of the Earth plane? Why in some cases do you need a translator?' This is a question which I am sure has puzzled many. I felt it necessary to communicate the reason why.

Because I am pure Spiritual energy, I do not have the normal consciousness of a soul on the Earth plane. I am one with what you know as God or the Ultimate Being. That energy and we, the Masters, have no personality, so to speak of. We are pure energy. It does not mean that we have no identity, but that we are not like the souls on the Earth plane. Ascended beings are different energies. Because we are Ascended, we cannot function on the Earth plane unless we use a channel. That channel is trained and developed to take the force of our energy and to be the spokesperson for us. We have no vocabulary, in our Spiritual world, there are no words spoken, because there are no physical bodies. Just the essence of energy.

In order for us to 'speak' on the Earth plane, we need to use the vocabulary and subconscious/conscious memory of those who we channel through. This procedure takes many years of Earth time to learn. Often, our channels have done this before in other incarnations, so it is easy for us to connect again. Until one is in the Spiritual world, one cannot understand the workings of this procedure. We become 'one' with our channels. We use their energy, they use ours. That is the reason why."

WHY DO YOU HAVE FEAR?

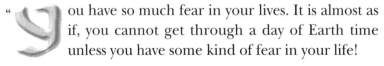 "ou have so much fear in your lives. It is almost as if, you cannot get through a day of Earth time unless you have some kind of fear in your life!

The recent eclipse of the Sun, was a good example of that. So many people were in fear of that eclipse and of the

Grand Cross that was to follow it. My channel was constantly asked, 'What will happen?' And through her I said, 'It will not be as bad as you fear.'

There have always been disasters, there always will be disasters. It is Nature working her renewal. Unlike humanity who fear change, Nature welcomes it and constantly renews itself. The terrible fate expected by many did not occur. 'Yes,' you can say, 'but there was an earthquake!' But there have always been earthquakes. The souls who left in that earthquake chose not to stay, as will many more souls in the future through other natural happenings.

What is wrong with dying and leaving the Earth plane? We rejoice when you come home. The souls who left have chosen to leave now. It is their choice. They are joyful to be reunited with their families in the Spirit realms.

If only humanity would understand and accept that each family member, husband, wife, child, is just another soul. If only they would see that person as a soul to learn lessons with. If only they would not cling to each other and have fear. It would make the transition of those souls leaving, and those souls losing a loved one, a lot better. For that is all you are to each other, souls helping each other to learn lessons. One day you will be reunited in the Spirit World, but not as you are on the Earth plane, just as souls.

There must be grief, it is natural in the human body to grieve, but grieve with love and happiness that the soul has returned to the Spirit World. Do not cling and have fear of never seeing them again. For what you fear, you will create. If that soul wishes to come back into your energy to let you know they have *only* passed over, and are still in consciousness, your fear will stop them.

All of the great Prophets have spoken of fear. Let go of yours, whatever it may be. Let go of any fear associated to the future of the Earth plane. I will say again, it will not be as bad as you think it will be."

WHY DO YOU LIE TO YOURSELF?

"Why do you lie to yourself? You say you are happy in your marriage, work, private life, yet you are not. You are in denial, and while you are in denial you cannot raise your vibration. In order to raise the vibration of one's energy, one needs to be honest with oneself. You *can* lie to yourself, but you *cannot* lie to the Ultimate Being. So many of you are living in fear. You stay in relationships, jobs, marriages, because of fear. You live a lie. You cannot be happy in a life where you are not at peace. To be at peace, means that you need to be honest with yourself and have no denial for your happiness. You say to yourself, 'Yes, I am happy,' but when we in the Spiritual realms look at your life, you are not.

Be honest with yourself, look at your life. If you have stress in your life; if you are in a relationship where you are not comfortable or happy; if you have a fear of loneliness, poverty, or any other negative emotion, you are not at peace. How can you be if your life is not happy?

Be true to yourself. First of all, admit where you are unhappy. Secondly, determine to do something about it. Thirdly, face the fear. Often the fear is nothing, and when

189

it is confronted, it disappears. Be true to yourself, stop lying to yourself, start the path to raising your vibration, to being happy and at peace. You can be you know!"

WHY I AM CALLED 'LORD MAITREYA'

"I have never wanted to be called Lord Maitreya. It is humanity who has done this. I have said many times, I am the teacher only. It is the message not the messenger. This applies to all of the Masters as well.

In the beginning, we were known simply as teachers from the Spiritual realms. Humanity though has labelled us 'Lords' in their desire to elevate us. We have not wanted elevation.

When I first channelled through this Medium, Margaret, I chose not to be known as Maitreya, but as an energy called Isaiah. However, because of this website and my work as a World Teacher, I needed to be known as Maitreya. 'Lord Maitreya' is what many souls know me as. This is not my desire, and never has been to be exalted, for I am not. Yes, I have Ascended. I no longer live on the Earth plane and I require a channel to bring my teachings through. However, I am simply only the teacher. The teacher of the world for those who wish to listen to those words and who wish to better their lives. I have chosen, from this Earth time forward, to answer any communications with the simple name Maitreya."

WHY ME?

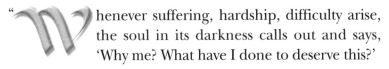

"henever suffering, hardship, difficulty arise, the soul in its darkness calls out and says, 'Why me? What have I done to deserve this?'

If the soul was in a state of permanent bliss and happiness, without strife or trouble, there would be no learning because these states do not allow for that. When there is peace and happiness there is just that. The purpose of the soul on the Earth plane is to grow and expand, to climb even higher and to free itself forever from the Earth plane. At times in this incarnation one can experience times of strife, loss of job for instance, financial restrictions, attack by those around one. When this happens, the Self is usually brought to the fore and starts to complain loudly, 'Why me?' being a usual question. Everything is looked at from a negative point of view. Rarely is the experience seen as an opportunity to change, or to move on from a situation that is stagnant or to move forward to bigger and better things. Yes, all that comes in the form of difficulty is a blessing, if only you can see that.

My channel, many years ago, went through a very difficult situation in which she lost her business, her marriage, and even found herself moving away from the country she lived in. She had been given warning through a reading that this would happen, but when it happened, she could only see the negative. Even at the airport waiting to leave the country she was still negative, saying, 'I can see nothing for myself in the new country.' Her negativity about the situation stopped her seeing her future and the opportunities which were there. That is why she could not see!

Nine months later, she had a new life, a very popular radio programme, a new career in journalism and much happiness. Her journey to another country had brought her much success and joy. Much more than had she stayed where she had been living.

Too often, humankind look to the negative when things happen, instead of looking to the positive. You always fear the worst, usually because that is all life has dealt you in the past, and because you have allowed only the negative in your life.

Try not to let adversity get you down. When it comes, look upon it as a friend who can give you a stepping stone to a better situation or vibration. There are no accidents, everything happens for a reason. It may be sad to leave things behind, move on, go through difficulty, as you see it, and have frustration in your life; but all of these issues allow the soul to grow, *if* the soul allows the changes to happen and does not fight. The more you fight, the more difficulty you will encounter.

If you look at the situation as a time to grow, move and expand your life, that is what you will draw into your energy, because your thoughts will create your reality. If you look upon the changes with fear, doubt, or any other negative emotion, then that is what you will draw into your energy, a negative situation.

Each soul in its lifetime will go through happiness and joy, sadness and sorrow, all of it designed to help the soul to grow and move on. Often adversity can be the result of past life actions, or because the soul has chosen it as a time to grow.

The story of the American couple in Italy, whose son was

shot and died as a result of this, is an example. They did not allow the death of their son to be a negative experience. In fact, they gave his body organs for donation so that others may live. In their time of sorrow, they thought not of themselves but of others. Truly a positive coming out of a negative.

The next time you find yourself having a little difficulty or hardship, instead of saying, 'why me?' ask yourself, 'what wonderful happening will occur because of this?' and then let it happen. It will you know!"

WHY NATURAL DISASTERS?

"*I* was recently asked, 'Why it is that the countries being affected by earthquakes, floods and other natural disasters are poor countries; when the rich countries, with crime and other material desires, are not touched?'

Life is constant change, but often, certain people or whole groups of people will not change. They live as if of yesterday. Their houses are the same as they were a hundred, even a thousand years ago, such as in the Middle Eastern countries on the Earth plane. It is Universal Law that all is constant change. Many souls are frightened to change. They fear change, just as people once feared a round Earth and continued to think it was flat!

When disaster strikes and brings catastrophic disaster, it is Nature's way of saying to humanity, 'If you will not change, we will change you.' This applies not only in a group sense, as in a certain area of a country, but also to

193

individual souls. The individuals who will not change and stay in their fear of change often find that they are forced to change. Fire, flood and natural disaster will force that change.

It is not the Divine Being who does this, but humanity itself. If all of humanity respected the Law of Change and had no fear, there would be no disasters; for all would be in harmony with the natural Universal Law. For each force, there is an equal and opposite force in the Universe. What man fears, he will bring into his energy. If a person fears their partner leaving them, they will create this. If people fear change, then the Universe will create change.

When humanity understands this Law, then and only then, will nature be able to balance itself. Only then will natural disaster cease. There is no need for it to happen, humanity with its fear creates its own downfall."

WHY
NEW ZEALAND?

"I am constantly asked, 'Master, why are you in New Zealand? Why did you choose to channel and work through Margaret from there? Why did my channel leave England and move a long distance to work with me?'

She was pre-destined to do it. We, on the Spiritual planes, chose New Zealand because of the energy and because it is the closest country to the first light of the Universe. When the rest of the world see the light, it has already shone in New Zealand. The first rays of the sun are very powerful, especially after the night. For those who receive those rays first, and those in New Zealand do, it can speed up their development on a Spiritual level.

The country has always been ecologically concerned. They were nuclear free. They take care of their land and the energy of New Zealand is one of the finest in the world. That is why we chose to teach from here and to communicate from here.

The country is untainted by commercialism. Children can still roam free in the streets. There is much to be said for the country and for those who come and learn with me; their development is enhanced by the energy.

Yes, I have taught in other places. This was to enable those in the northern hemisphere to channel my energy and the energy of the Masters there. I will continue to travel with my channel and teach in other countries, but for those who come to New Zealand, they will feel the energy and it will enhance their studies."

WORKING WITH THE MASTERS

" I am often asked, 'Master, how can I work with you and the Masters?' I tell those souls, you can do so, but by doing so one has to give up the Self. The Self is the logic which is always giving you answers. It has an answer for everything and always feels that it is right. When one joins with us in the Spiritual realms, one cannot do what you or the Self wants to do. One then has to listen to our requests. Our requests may not come directly from us, but through others.

For many incarnations the Self has been in control. *It* has made the decisions. But *now*, we ask you to follow our directions, to listen to what we wish for you to do. We do this in order that you may grow and expand the soul. Your Self becomes indignant at this and wants to do what it has done for so many incarnations; it is at this moment in your soul growth that many souls stop growing. They cannot see the reason behind our actions, and anyway, 'Why should I listen to you?' It is at this crucial time that many souls fall by the wayside and fail yet again.

Letting go of your own logic and having acceptance of what is given to you is the first step in Spiritual growth. Many would say that this is manipulation. My channel's husband was told many times by well-meaning souls that he was being manipulated by we, the Masters, because he listened to us and not to his Self, or others like themselves. Yet in seven Earth years he has grown spiritually, the equivalent of one thousand lives. Is this manipulation?

We want to help you and the Earth plane to grow spiritually. But to do so, if you are to grow personally, this means listening to us and to our instructions in any form.

'How will I know it is not my Self telling me this?' you may ask. Because we will ask you through a channel or in the highest form of meditation or in your dreams. It will be in your heart that you will feel this prompting. When it is there, it is from us.

When it comes from the mind it comes from the Self, when it comes from the heart it is from the Divine."

WORRY

"There is so much worry on the Earth plane today. Worry over money, relationships, life in general. It has become a major issue in the life of many. You can say to me, 'But Master, you do not live on the Earth plane or have the problems that we encounter.' No we do not, that is true. However, we also know that every time you worry about anything you stop the flow, not only for yourself, but for others. For worry is a negative thought.

When you worry, you set off a negative energy pattern. What is worse is that, you do not realize that when you worry about another, about their welfare, that you also stop the flow of energy for them. Yes you do!

You create a block which if not removed can stop another person from experiencing their life lessons. If a person that you know, say your son or daughter, friend or whomever it may be, has good karma and is on the Earth plane to experience wonderful things in life, by worrying about them, you can actually stop that from happening. Think about that! Think of the times each day you worry about other people. What is worse, is that all that energy spent on worrying about others, takes energy away from yourself. You not only can stop others from using their energy, but you also stop your own flow.

Every soul is meant to have abundance in their life. Yet, so many of you stop the flow of that abundance on all levels, by worrying about things which often never happen. It is difficult to stop worrying. It takes discipline to stop the flow of negative thought, but it can be done. It can be

197

done by affirmation, and it can be done by being aware of your thought pattern.

Each day, as you worry, as you realize that you *do* worry, *are* worrying, say to yourself, 'I am stopping the flow either for myself, or for the person I am worrying about.' Then watch the situation change. You will be quite amazed!"

YOU ARE ON A JOURNEY

"You are on a journey, you started it at birth. You can either make the journey a hard one or make it easy. *You* hold the key! *You* make the choices!

Life does not have to be difficult. *You* make it difficult with your stubbornness, pride, ego and Self. How do you want your life to be? If you do not want the struggle, then ask the Universe to help you and then slowly, watch your life change and become better. It will not happen overnight, but it will happen. However, *you* need to let go and let the Universe lead you with no fear or doubt, just total trust!

I have said many times to my students, you were all born with an Aladdin's lamp, you have just forgotten how to rub it!"

YOU CANNOT TAKE ANYTHING WITH YOU

"In the year 2000, as I channel this information, the Earth plane is in turmoil in certain parts of the world with war and fighting. The war is based on either religion or land. What the souls involved in these actions do not realize is that, when they pass into the Spiritual realms, after they are dead physically, they can take nothing with them. What is the point of fighting for land, fighting because one's belief is not the same as yours? When, in the final outcome, the land will *never* be yours! The people will *never* believe what you believe for each soul has its own personal beliefs, because every soul is an individual.

Humanity spends years of Earth time fighting for what they feel they believe is wrong, but what is wrong? No soul has the answer. I wrote in a previous message that each man has his own truth. The war in the Middle East has been going on for centuries, land is won and land is lost. A piece of dirt belongs to one country and then it is taken back and belongs to another. All this in the name of religion, greed or ego. What a waste of energy; yet they cannot see that it is a waste of energy.

It is time for humanity to understand that you come into this world, this Earth plane, with nothing. You leave with nothing. What you have in between birth and death is there to use, on loan so to speak, for your incarnation. It can either be used in a positive way, or it can be used in a negative way. You choose! Let the choosing be in peace and productive endeavours, not for war, ego, greed, fear

199

or any other negative emotion. It is time to stop the war, stop the killing, stop the greed, and understand that all that you fight for, all that you argue over, is not taken with you when you return home to the Spiritual world. What is taken back with you is the negative actions you have used, and the reaction to that is karma which needs to be repaid.

Many souls say, 'Why do I suffer in my life?' We in Spirit say at that time, look at your past actions!"

YOUR FEAR!

"Where does your fear come from? Think about this question? Where *does* it come from? If you have a fear of anything, then there has to be a beginning for that fear, it just did not come from nowhere.

Fear is energy, it is a trapped energy. So, you are trapped by your fear. Many incarnations can pass where you have the same fear. It travels with you like an overcoat, incarnation after incarnation. Life after life you run away from it despite we, in the Spiritual World, bringing that fear into your life to assist you to free yourselves from it. Once it is faced, then it no longer has any power over you and you are free.

Where are your fears? How long have you been running away from them, and how many incarnations have passed since your fears began? These questions are very important, so why not face the fears you have now?

Remember that we are just waiting for your request for

assistance. We will be there to help you to face your fears and remove them from your life altogether. It may take some Earth time, but one day, little by little, you will take the giant leap and completely conquer all fear. What a joyous day!"

YOUR LIFE JOURNEY!

"Y ou think you are alone on your journey on this Earth plane. Yet, you are surrounded by hundreds of souls who help you along that journey and who care so very much about you. You call out in the despair. You have said yourself, 'Why do you do this to me?' Yet you do not realize you do it to yourself!

All of your suffering is chosen, *yes!* To many this may seem terrible. 'How can we choose such terrible experiences?' I can hear you state. You do not realize that it is but an illusion, it is an experience only, it is not real. It *seems* real, and everything on the Earth plane makes it look real, but only when one has raised the vibration and moved away from the Earth existence, can one see through the illusion. It is your emotional body, your fear, doubt, insecurity and other emotions which keep you in the illusion. You think what you have is reality, but in effect, it is all illusion and only when you come home to us, can you see through that.

Do you think we enjoy watching you suffer? Do you think we enjoy watching your pain and your life experiences? No we do not! We feel all that you do and more. We have deep compassion for all who experience pain and

201

suffering and do all we can to assist in giving healing and spiritual support to those who need it. Each one of you has many souls on our side of the veil, who help you in your times of need and pain and suffering.

However, we cannot interfere with your destiny, the path you have chosen. Yes, *you* have chosen. Nobody else can be blamed for your life experiences, all was chosen before birth. Once you can accept and understand this, then life itself becomes easier; the struggle, not so hard. There is an understanding of life and destiny.

One cannot, at this stage, see through the illusion, but one has an understanding of it to enable one to move forward, to see through it. Do not blame anyone else for your problems in life. Do not blame the energy you know as God, *so many* do!

This energy loves you, knows every soul, their destiny and life path. Once you can control the emotional body, the mental body and look within, all the answers are there as to how, why, who and what. We have so much love for you, it is *you* however, who often do not have the love for us!"

Appendices

Appendix 1

Transcript of the United Nations SEAT Speech by Maitreya
Page 205

Appendix 2

DISASTER IN THE USA and THE HALL OF MIRRORS – Re: 9/11
Page 215

Appendix 1

Transcript of the United Nations SEAT Speech by Maitreya

SEAT stands for Society for Enlightenment and Transformation. It is a group within the United Nations that comes under the United Nations Staff Recreational Council. SEAT is involved in prayer groups and other activities that help a positive outcome in the work of the UN around the world.

The Master was invited by the President of SEAT, Jennifer Borchers, to speak to their group at the United Nations on the 8th June 1999. The talk began at 1:15pm and lasted for 40 minutes. Around 40 people were present. (English transcription by Pablo Romero).

* * * * *

UNITED NATIONS –
SEAT Speech

"Good day to you. What a joy to be here in this energy that you have so graciously provided today."

The Spiritual work is one that is not easy to do, for there is so much darkness in the world today. You can say to yourselves, 'But what can I do? I am so little a person! I am nobody! What can my influence do to change humanity to a more enlightened being?' And I will say to you, 'Where you are gathered either one or more, and you have the name of your God, your Spirit, you are one with Creation. You are one with Love. You are one with the Divine. You are one with The Universal Brotherhood. Your thoughts, everything that you think, becomes. If you think of peace, eventually, the more people that think of peace, the more will be transformed and the more that will be energized.

Each one of you here in this room has the ability to create peace in your meditations. By thinking and meditating on peace in your prayers and in your daily thoughts, it is possible to change the energy of the world. It may seem such a hard task, especially those of you who work in this building, for not only is there conflict in the world, but there are many who have conflicts with the United Nations. Many who do not have nice thoughts at all about what happens here.

They are not educated. They do not see the hard work

and the effort, the energy, the love that is provided here by so many in such difficult circumstances. Where war reigns, hardship and difficulty are a part of life. The energy of those who work here is a very precious energy. There's no material reward, no glory, no glamour, just hard work, and yet so many choose to do the work of Spirit through this organization. Each one of you, with your thoughts, with your prayers and your meditation, can change humanity's thinking. When you link with us, we not only use our energy but yours as well. We use the energy of the universe and we link it with yours. Humanity is not yet at a stage where there is total peace in the world, for the Ego reigns supreme and the Self is important, not the Higher Self. Many Souls do not know they even have a Higher Self. They look around with their heads buried in the sand, they cannot see and do not often wish to see. But the energy that is in the world, at this point of time, is shifting and changing the way society lives and thinks.

Think back to 50 Earth years ago and to how Spirit was represented then. Think of Now, of all of the 'New Age,' as you call it, in bookshops and on television programmes. Television personalities teaching of the Spiritual, videos, cassettes, as well as people who offer their services to channel. It has changed in 50 Earth years so much. It has changed and will continue to change, for humanity is finally raising the vibrations of the Earth plane.

You may see yourselves as inconsequential, a little person, an unimportant being, and yet, you are so important to the Plan. For what you think, what you create, you will manifest. It has been said so often in this building and around the world, that education is the key. And

207

education of the Spiritual is more important also. You know of your body, you know of your minds, but so very few know of your Soul. So few understand the Spiritual. It is still classed as 'evil' to be able to prophesy, to be able to heal. Many look upon the Spiritual gifts as alien, yet each one of you in this room has the ability to prophesy, and to heal, and to manifest peace.

If you could see the energy that surrounds each and every one of you, you would be surprised, very surprised. When humanity understands the Spiritual, then humanity will be able to create peace. I am not saying that it is the most important factor for there is the body, the mind, and the soul, but it is important that credence be given to the Spiritual.

Long ago, the American Red Indians understood the Soul and the Spiritual. Many cultures around the world have also understood the soul and the Spiritual, but it has been hidden. It has been removed from your learning and teaching for so long. Humanity is ready now and becoming more ready to learn of the Spiritual worlds. I say to each one of you to speak of Spiritual worlds whenever you can. You can say, 'Oh, but I told my neighbour and she did not want to listen,' but how do you know that you have not sowed the seed? You can sow seeds in Africa, and it may stay in the ground for twenty Earth years never to grow. And then, one day, it grows into a huge field of corn, or a huge tree. That is what you can do when you speak of Spiritual things to those you know and those you do not know. You sow a seed. The seed may not sprout for many years. You often think you are wasting your time by sowing seeds, by telling people of Spiritual

Realms especially when they look at you as if you're weird.
They don't want to know, but if you sow the seed at least it
has been planted, waiting to grow. Whether it grows
immediately, or in five, ten, twenty, or even fifty Earth
years, you have done something. You may not see the
fruits of your labours immediately, but you at least, have
done something. Never think that your words have not
been useful, for they have been; will be. And if you give
the message, it may manifest now, or later to help
humanity. For each soul there is a time of awakening.
There is a time when it finally sees the Light and decides
to grow. That is when that person's seed grows; the seed
that was planted there by somebody else.

Never think that your words go in vain, for they do not.
You sow seeds. You are farmers sowing your seeds,
planting your fields for the future. If you touch one soul
with your words, then your life has been worth living. You
can say that you have done something with your life. Each
one of you has a bag of seeds, each one of you can sow
those seeds. It is such a glorious thing to be able to speak
of Spiritual realms. Next time somebody speaks to you of
the Spiritual, watch their eyes, watch their faces, for they
fill with energy. The eyes light up, and inner peace fills
the Soul.

For so long now, humanity has been denied the Spiritual.
Conditioning, religion, repression, all and more, have
stopped humanity from finding out about the Spiritual
realms in the true sense. What is Spiritual? I am often
asked, 'What is the Divine?' It is pure Love. It is
unconditional, non-judgmental acceptance of each soul
for who it is; not judging colour, race, personal traits,

209

history or rank. It is loving your brother, your sister. It is being at peace with others.

When you are with the Spiritual worlds, you have no desire to gossip, for gossip is judgmental. Yes, when you speak of another you judge another. It is being in love with the universe and the universal energy. To love others you must love yourself, yet so many people judge themselves! 'Oh I am too fat! I am too thin! I have a long nose! My body is wobbly!' You judge yourself so harshly. Each one of you is who you are because of your genetic make-up. But when you leave your body and return to the Spiritual realms, you are perfect. When you are on this Earth plane, in your body, you are perfect. You just cannot see it, for you judge yourselves so harshly. You can love, but to love others, you must love yourself.

You must be at peace, not only with others, but with yourself. I am often asked, 'Master, what can I do to become Spiritual? Tell me the tricks, tell me how to do it.' And I say, it's very simple, love yourself. Love who you are, with your wobbly body, your long nose, your extra weight or your thinness. It does not matter, your body is just a vehicle. It is only a vehicle. It carries the soul, and it is the way it is, because of your genetic make-up. Stop judging yourselves, allow yourselves to be the perfection you are destined to be, you should be. Stop thinking that you are anything less. When you do this, you will find that you will be at peace. You will find that when you stop judging yourselves, all around you becomes beautiful. Yes, yes it can and will.

Another area that you don't understand a great deal, is

how you use your own energy, the energy of the Spiritual. So many of you become hurt, so many of you allow others to upset you, allow others to create disharmony in your life and yet, if you do not give anything any energy, it cannot affect you. So many of you say, 'Oh, but my friend, husband, lover, mother, sister, brother, father is so powerful, I am afraid of them,' and yet the only power that they have is the power that you give them. Think about it. When you take back your power, they are usually so shocked. I say to those who have difficulty communicating, 'Speak your truth quietly and clearly.' You don't have to yell, shout or argue. What is wrong with saying, 'I am sorry, that is your vision, not mine. I'm sorry, I disagree with you.' Yet so many of you in this room are frightened to do just that. You are entitled to speak your truth to another, as long as you do not choose violence or anger. Just speak your truth and release the throat chakra energy. You will speak a lot better if you do so.

The next time your work mate or your friend or your partner or close associate or family create disharmony in your life, instead of giving it energy and reacting as most people do, don't react. Just don't react! You will be amazed at how, when you do not react, the situation will change. Violence begets violence, anger begets anger and frustration begets frustration. What a waste of energy! Try changing your life, try changing your thinking. These are little things to inform you about which can have a profound effect on your life. If you have fear of speaking, in speaking your truth quietly and clearly, all that you have to do is to ask we in Spirit before you open your mouth. All you have to do is ask us, 'Divine Spirit, please help me to speak to this person in truth and love, without anger,

211

frustration or indifference, or any of the other negative emotions,' and we will be at your side. We promise you, we will place into your mind, words for you to say, and you'll find that your mouth will open and you will say your words. It will be as if a great weight is lifted from you, for you will finally express yourself.

It is this that we, in Spirit, are here to bring you the message of. To educate humanity to let go of emotion, to let go of anger and frustration. There are alternatives. They can be used, they have been used and they are successful. Each one of you has so much inside of you, so much love, understanding and compassion. Each one of you has the ability to change the Earth plane, to change the thinking, even as small as you are. History is full of people who were nobody, yet who did great things. Over the next ten Earth years much change will come to the Earth plane. Much has been made of 'doom and gloom,' that the Earth is going to end and negative things will happen. Rubbish, nonsense is what I say! Those are my channel's words, not mine. I have to use her words, for in Spiritual Realms we do not have words, we have thoughts. It is the only word I can think to use that speaks of the truth.

Have no fear of the future of the Earth plane, Yes, there will be war and earthquakes and floods as there have been for aeons of time. But you see, the Earth plane is changing, humanity is changing. More and more people become what you call 'Light Workers.' The more and more people love themselves, more and more people speak their truth, more and more people sow their seeds, the more enlightened the world will become. From one acorn an oak tree grows. Think about it. Each one of you is an acorn. Each one of you is a seed. Each one of you has such a desire to serve humanity and we can help you to do that. And how do you do that?

You join with us in Spirit. In meditations you ask us to enter. In your prayers you ask us to help. But more than anything, love yourselves, with all its wobbly bits! Your body is the most precious vessel for it holds your soul. Nobody ever sees themselves as perfect, ever! There's no perfection in any human being! But in the soul there is always perfection. Always there is perfection.

I am just a messenger. That is my role as a teacher. The website that I persuaded my channel's ex-husband to found, to create, has over seventy countries who regularly view the writings of the Spiritual Realms. It is called, 'The Lord Maitreya Site,' but it holds the writings of many ascended beings, not just those of myself. And more and more, each day, each month, each year, more countries look at this site and gain, hopefully, an insight and a message from the writings thereon.

With us doing our part and with you doing your part, each one of you sowing seeds; with us shaking the tree and letting the seeds drop, what a wonderful energy we have for the future of humanity! Yes it is hard work. There is no glamour. It is hard work wading through the mud of negativity on this Earth plane, but we can raise the vibration. We can raise the energy so that, not too far in the future, humanity will no longer wish to be at war. There will be no famine, poverty, hardship, difficulty, and it will all come with education, as simple as that.

Education of the body, education of the mind, education of the Spiritual realms. The three combined.

There have been many Prophets who have brought the message of Spirit to the Earth plane, and they will continue to come. We will continue to send them until humanity has raised its vibration, but the message is just love. Love yourself and you can love others. Love yourself, and you are on your way to finding peace within.

It is time, now, for me to retire. I thank you for giving me the opportunity to speak the truth of the Divine. Whether it be your truth or not, each one of you is a seed for love. Each one of you can go and sow those seeds. I ask you to consider to do so.

In the name of the Divine Light of Spiritual Realms, I bless you, thank you, and embrace you. Good Day."

Maitreya

Appendix 2

DISASTER IN THE USA and THE HALL OF MIRRORS

"At this time of tragedy in the USA, I have been asked if I will comment on what happens to people who commit atrocities when they die. First of all, you must understand that the Self does not reside in the Spiritual body, but in the physical. The Higher Self is of the Spiritual. When a soul passes out of the physical body, there is no Self (Ego) anymore. When a soul arrives in the World of Spirit, usually they are quite confused because our world is very much like your world, the difference being that our world is more real!

It is normal for the soul to have a period of rest when they arrive, because many souls have a traumatic death, and find it difficult to believe that they are indeed alive in the Spiritual Realms, or as many believe it, 'Heaven.' After a period of rest, the soul is taken by their Guardian Spirit to a Hall of Mirrors. (A Guardian is the Spiritual being who is with you from birth until death on the physical plane). This is a room where the soul stands in front of a giant mirror and has to face themselves. Their whole life is shown to them. They not only see what they did to others, but they also feel the emotion and trauma that the other person felt. It is at this time that many souls become extremely saddened and ashamed, because they see all that they have done, the good and the bad. Usually, at this stage, the soul does not want to move on, and will make a request to contact one in the physical world whom they knew, family member, friend, etc, to give a message, or, to

215

say they are very sorry for what they did. This has to be arranged from Spirit and a medium or channel found to act as the messenger, but it is allowed. The soul usually cannot rest until it has made its apology or given its message. Once it has done so, it can then rest and return to Spirit in its fullness before it returns to the Earth plane by being born again. It then goes over into Spirit fully. While it is waiting for the channel/medium to be found, the soul usually works in the reception areas in a humanitarian way. This is one way of repaying karma.

Nobody escapes the Hall of Mirrors, nobody. I will tell you now; they are often totally devastated souls when they return from this place. Much comfort has to be given to them afterwards for many cannot believe what they have done.

One cannot go further into the true realms of Spirit until one has been to the Hall of Mirrors. In light of the tragedy which happened in the Earth year 2001, in the month of September, on the 11th, I will attest to you that the souls responsible for the tragedy and for the loss of life are so deeply upset at their actions that they are now in deep shock. Know this, as you condemn those responsible. Think also of the karma that has now been generated for this action. It will surely come back onto them in a future incarnation.

The souls responsible were given the impression that it should be done for God. I will tell you now that God, who is pure Love, would never condone what took place.

This is my testament in truth on this matter."

Maitreya

Glossary

Ascension The soul's final transition to Heaven

Astral Plane "Is the sum total of all that is. It is the place where Angels and workers in the Angelic Realms reside to watch over the Universe. Man/woman, or rather their souls, can enter this plane and see for themselves the wonders available to the human being if only they would ask." Channelled answer. Publishers Note: Readers can do this by learning to Astral Project.

Aura Every living creature has an energy field surrounding their body. This field is called the aura and with practice, we can see it, feel it and describe it.

Chakra Points on the body where energy enters and leaves the human body. There are seven main ones.

Chiron Is an asteroid travelling in orbit between Saturn and Uranus. In your birth chart, Chiron represents your deeper sense of purpose, and adds a subtle yet powerful drive to achieve a connection to higher values.

Dwjhal Kuhl	An Ascended Master. He was Casper, one of the three wise men who attended the birth of Jesus, and Johann Sebastian Bach in former lives.
Etheric Web	Web-like, light emanating threads of energy in the auric field
Ezekiel's Wheel	From the Old Testament, Ezekiel saw a vision of a burning wheel containing four creatures each with four heads.
Karma	The sum of a person's actions in previous states of existence, viewed as deciding his or her fate after death. Also common to Hinduism and Buddhism.
Kundalini	An energy that passes through, and links together, the seven chakras in the human body producing a state of bliss and enlightenment.
Madame Blavatsky	see www.blavatskytrust.org.uk
Natal Chart	This charts your life plan, based on the time & date of your birth.
Transmuted	Change the form, nature or substance of. i.e. change your anger (negative energy) into love (positive energy).

Spiritual Philosophy Publishing

Spiritual Philosophy has a mission. Our principal aim is to give first time writers the opportunity to get their books into print.

We want to encourage people of every age, gender, race and religious persuasion to read our very special books and to extract those teachings that feel right for them as individuals.

Every single person on this planet is important. It is for each person to develop himself or herself spiritually and it is for each person to find his or her own truth.

Many, many people are depressed, lonely and often question the reason for being on this planet. Through our books, we aim to help each person enjoy life and understand the wonder in balancing their material lives with their Spiritual role. When the two are in balance, life is simply wonderful.

God bless you and welcome to our family of friends.

Visit us at:

www.spiritualphilosophy.co.uk

or write to:

Kevin Brookes
Spiritual Philosophy Publishing
PO Box 79
Midhurst
West Sussex GU29 9WW

www.maitreya-edu.org

In 1996
Margaret Birkin and **Peter Luke**
started this website
at the request of **Maitreya**.

Margaret has been a channel and clairvoyant for 25 years, and has written for magazines, as well as newspapers. Also she has been a very successful radio clairvoyant. In 1999 she channeled a speech with Maitreya to a special group of Spiritual people at the UN in New York. Margaret has written a number of books which are available on the website, and travels around the world taking the Master's teaching. Also she is now an accomplished esoteric astrologer, and corporate clairvoyant/speaker.

Peter Luke began his career in electronics but changed direction in 1992 when he met Margaret and formed a Spiritual partnership with her. He was the main founder of the website in 1996. Most of the instruction for this site was done intuitively. Peter is also an accomplished past life therapist and healer.

Both of them now dedicate their lives to Maitreya's work. "It is our passion," Margaret has said. They have created the Australian Institute of Metaphysics with a retail gallery next to it, which is situated on Tamborine Mountain in Queensland, Australia, and are presently creating a school in New Zealand.

They also have some volunteers who help them with translations on the site. Ratna Colluru and Mark King assist Peter with the more technical parts of the web servers, plus general html programming. Without these volunteers you would not see the website you see today.

Listen to Margaret's radio interview on Evolution Radio, including a deep trance message from Maitreya.

http://www.mastery-of-life.com/radio/Margaret_ Part_ 1.mp3
http://www.mastery-of-life.com/radio/Margaret_ Part_ 2.mp3
http://www.mastery-of-life.com/radio/Margaret_ Part_ 3.mp3
http;//www.mastery-of-life.com/radio/Margaret_ Part_ 4.mp3

Courses in the UK

In 2004 Maitreya spoke directly to Jacquie Verbeek and asked her to start a school in England. She took up the challenge and now teaches his work in the UK. Her courses cover: levels of awareness, the Self & Higher Self, past lives therapy, meditation, self development, the creation of total inner peace and manifesting all that you need in life.

Contact Jacquie Verbeek through her website:

www.masteryourlife.co.uk

Are you aged 16 – 30 years and questioning your life? Are you searching but do not know exactly what *you* want? Then watch out for our first novel, a Spiritual adventure:

Some Silent Hero

Author: Stephanie Brookes, at 24 years, is probably one of the youngest writers in the Mind, Body & Spirit genre. She finished the script one day after her graduation ceremony at Portsmouth University in July 2004. She aims to travel and live on the west coast of America & Canada to research and write the second book, 'The Chief's Forgotten Land,' later this year.

The Book: Viv is struggling with an unhappy home life and no sense of purpose. She decides to take responsibility for her life and experiences the joys of synchronicity as she embraces the concept of Spirit. David, a mysterious biker and Spiritual Medium, enters her life and offers to help unravel the secrecy surrounding the death of her father. Their journey to America is shadowed by a young girl in Spirit.

Look out for our upcoming titles:

Sequel to "Some Silent Hero"

The Chief's Forgotten Land

Stephanie Brookes

Viv has changed; she has a newfound belief in herself. While her family want her to return home to England, her guide assures her that, at this point in time, she might wish to stay in America. Synchronicity and a compelling urge to experience the ancient wisdoms of the North American Indian tribes lead her north to the lands of the giant Redwoods. Here she meets a Shaman who tells her he has been waiting many, many years for her to come to him.

* * * * * * * * * * * * * *

A UK and World Debut:

Maitreya

Messages from the Master

Volume II

Channelled by Margaret Birkin.

In Volume I, Maitreya gave us his teachings to help mankind rediscover its connection with the Divine Spirit, God. In Margaret's second book, Maitreya gives us guidance to help each one of us in our daily lives. He talks about the human conditions, creating abundance, eliminating world poverty, education, business, religion, sexual repression, stem cells, abortion, love, world peace and simply having fun. All of the messages are given to uplift and encourage. There is nothing of the negative only of the positive. It will change the lives of everyone that reads it.

* * * * * * * * * * * * * * * *

Stepping Stones

Channelled by Desiréé Jestico

Desiréé's gift, her talent, her uniqueness as an individual is to give every speaker, in every School, in every Country, in every Church irrespective of creed, a wonderful, inspirational set of lessons that will captivate every listener with its messages of positive enlightenment. The teachings are from the Higher Spirits of Love & Light which treat every man, woman and child everywhere in the world with total equality. They will make you cry, they will make you laugh, they will make you tingle with hope and they will console you and comfort you. They will give you peace. These messages are for you.

* * * * * * * * * * * * * *